HOUSES OF New England

HOUSES OF New England

Peter T. Mallary
PHOTOGRAPHS BY Graydon Wood

THAMES AND HUDSON

This book was designed and produced
by John Calmann and Cooper Ltd, London

Designer: Gail Engert

First published in the USA in 1984
by Thames and Hudson Inc.,
500 Fifth Avenue, New York, New York 10110

ISBN: 0-500-01336-5

Library of Congress Catalog Card Number: 83-51864

Filmset by SX Composing Ltd
Origination by Peak Litho Plates Ltd
Printed in Italy by Canale SpA

1. (*Frontispiece*) Handsome railing distinguishes
the John Paul Jones House in Portsmouth,
New Hampshire.

Contents

Introduction

2, 3 A fireplace in the Gardner-Pingree House parlor with fine design motifs by Samuel McIntire. Note in particular the basket of fruit, McIntire's signature. The front door of Tate House (*below*) has the oldest fanlight in Portland.

Houses have stories to tell. This has been the guiding force in the choices represented in this book. An architectural history in its purest form might have omitted many of the houses discussed here and included others not mentioned, just as a volume of purely social history would have caused other changes. What I have striven for is to include houses that cover both aspects. Tate House in Portland is a perfect example. Architecturally it is fine, though overwhelmingly derivative (like most New England houses), and historically it tells the story of a man not widely known even in Maine. In bringing the various strands together I have touched on subjects ranging from the transposition of architectural styles from England to the frontier coast of Maine, to the history of the early settlements, and stories of the mast trade, Falmouth, and Captain Tate. The front door of Tate House opens on to more than its fine entry; it opens a chapter of New England history. Hunter House, Webb House, and the John Paul Jones House may have superficial resemblances, but each one tells a different story. Hunter House gives an insight into the lifestyle of Newport's early merchant princes, while Webb House is more than just a house where George Washington stayed – it was also the scene of historic discussions. The John Paul Jones house tells of the sad end of the Chevalier's American naval career and of the intricacies of Revolutionary politics. Each house reveals something slightly different about its world.

Harriet Thomas once spoke of historic houses in terms with which I wholeheartedly concur. She asked, "Just how does a house feel that has passed through ... almost three hundred years of joy and sorrow, trouble and change? For houses are living things. They speak the thoughts and picture the souls of those that occupy them." This seemingly somewhat romantic notion is borne out absolutely in the best of houses. A house like Gore Place is redolent with the presence of its first owners, an open and inviting place, while the Fairbanks House and the early section of the Wells-Thorn House reflect the travail of frontier life in their close quarters.

Needless to say such diversity requires a different approach for each house. Some will stress architectural features, while in others historical questions are preeminent, but the hope is that the overall brew is a satisfactory concoction. Some of the choices are personal; I picked certain houses because I like them. One of the dangers in tackling such fertile ground while limiting one's choice to twenty-four houses is that it gives

4–6 The entry hall (*left*) in Hunter House, with
the back door (formerly the front door) opening
out on to the harbor. (*above*) View through the
upstairs rooms in the 1751 portion of the Wells–
Thorn House and (*right*) the pantry in the 1717
section of the house.

rise to the question "Why this house and not that one?" D.C. Somerville once called historical analysis a process of "wholesale discarding," and this certainly applies here. There are no houses after 1850 – apart from The Elms in Newport – largely because, though there were many worthy candidates, I felt they said less about New England's history than a number of their earlier counterparts. The Elms has a place because a house from the grand era of Newport society seemed essential to complete the story of one of New England's most fascinating towns. I must fall back on Somerville's conclusion that while admitting the necessity of discarding he always hoped he had kept the right card.

7 The drawing room of The Elms. The Aubusson and the furniture are the original pieces gathered for the house when it was completed in 1901.

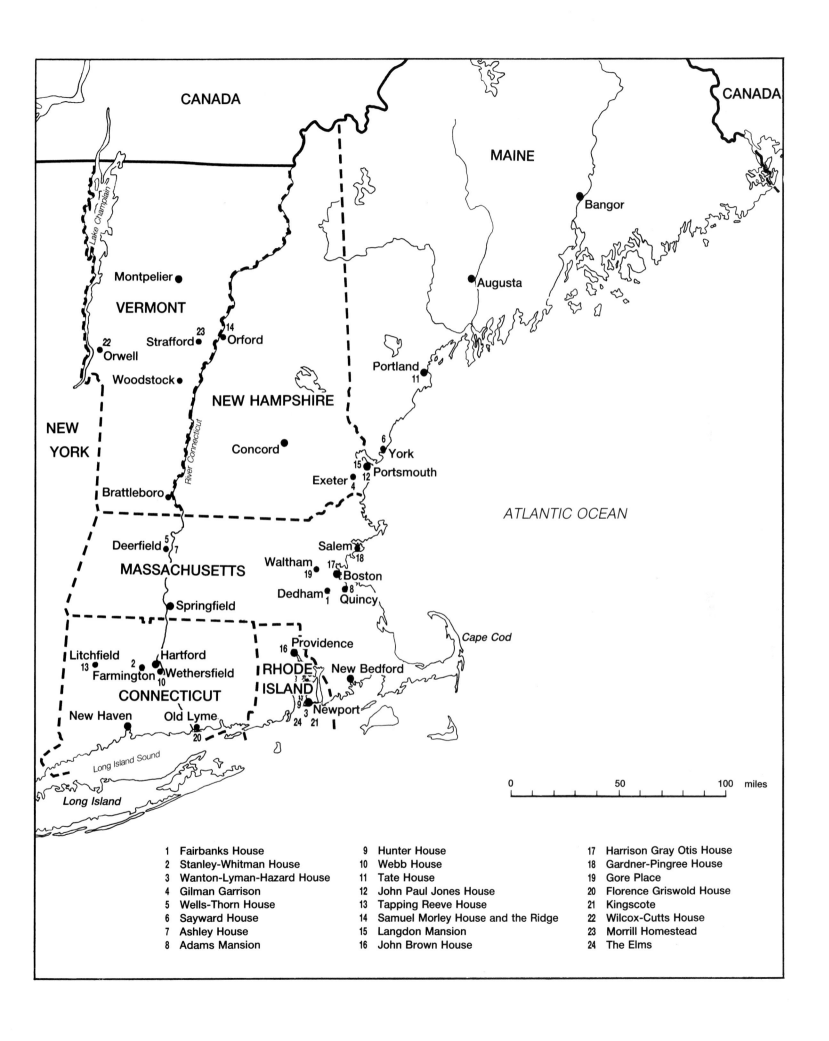

CANADA

CANADA

MAINE

Lake Champlain

● Bangor

● Montpelier

● Augusta

VERMONT

22 ● Orwell   Strafford ● 23   14 ● Orford

Portland
11

● Woodstock

NEW HAMPSHIRE

River Connecticut

NEW YORK

● Concord

6
York ●

15   ● Portsmouth

Exeter ●   12
4

Brattleboro ●

ATLANTIC OCEAN

Deerfield ● 5
7

Salem ●

18

MASSACHUSETTS

Waltham ●   17
19   ● Boston

Dedham ●   8
1   ● Quincy

● Springfield

Cape Cod

Litchfield ●   Hartford ●
13   2
Farmington ●   ● Wethersfield
10

16   Providence ●

RHODE
ISLAND   ● New Bedford

CONNECTICUT

New Haven ●   Old Lyme
20

3   ● Newport
24   21

Long Island Sound

Long Island

0   50   100   miles

1	Fairbanks House	9	Hunter House	17	Harrison Gray Otis House
2	Stanley-Whitman House	10	Webb House	18	Gardner-Pingree House
3	Wanton-Lyman-Hazard House	11	Tate House	19	Gore Place
4	Gilman Garrison	12	John Paul Jones House	20	Florence Griswold House
5	Wells-Thorn House	13	Tapping Reeve House	21	Kingscote
6	Sayward House	14	Samuel Morley House and the Ridge	22	Wilcox-Cutts House
7	Ashley House	15	Langdon Mansion	23	Morrill Homestead
8	Adams Mansion	16	John Brown House	24	The Elms

The New England ethos is one of the most enduring of American traditions. It is a hardy mixture of rugged individualism and carefully observed ritual. While Jamestown may predate Plymouth, and Philadelphians may claim greater cultural heritage than Bostonians, the traditions of the colonies northeast of New York have spread more pervasively in America than those of any other region.

Within the New England framework one encounters remarkable variety. In the decorative arts, for example, the region has produced work ranging from the simple and brilliantly painted Hadley chest, to the sculpted craftsmanship of an eighteenth-century Townsend-Goddard lowboy. New England's architecture reveals similar diversity, from the simple practicality of the Sayward House in Maine, to the elegance of the John Brown House in Providence, and the aristocratic charm of Boston's townhouses. A brief review of these styles may help the reader to place the houses in their proper architectural context.

When the first New England colonists arrived their chief and immediate concern was survival. Prior to the building of frame houses many settlers lived in huts or tents, which were more like certain rude dwellings in their English homeland than Indian wigwams. However, the settlers quickly availed themselves of America's greatest resource – tall standing timber. In his book *The Framed Houses of Massachusetts Bay, 1625–1725*, Abbot Cummings has traced the origin of many of these colonists to areas in England where wood-framed houses were commonplace and so the transfer of skills to the new environment was natural.

The seventeenth-century frame houses were simple, usually consisting of a few rooms surrounding a central chimney, or a side chimney and even fewer rooms, as was common in the famous salt-box design. Their architectural significance lies largely in their practical solutions to environmental difficulties. The Fairbanks, Stanley-Whitman, and Wanton-Lyman-Hazard houses are good examples of the central chimney plan. These early colonial houses were on the whole a simple reflection of English styles, but they are remarkable for their durability. They retained their popularity throughout the eighteenth century. The front portion of the Wells-Thorn House is a classic example of how, in 1751, a house of this basic type could incorporate the changes brought about by Georgian tastes, such as the replacement of casement windows with sashed ones.

The colonial Georgian era, lasting basically from 1720 to 1780, saw radical changes in the colonists' approach to architecture. The central chimney plan was opened up to allow for a large central entry hall or passageway, with rooms leading off the corridor. This necessitated the use of two chimneys, but allowed a more varied and interesting utilization of space. These developments were gradual. As European design books found their way to the Colonies, American Georgian houses incorporated their patterns and became increasingly ornate. This colonial adaptation and interpretation of European styles, manifest in both architecture and furniture, has a straightforward sturdy quality which is uniquely American. Paneled interior walls gave way to wainscoting with wallpaper above,

8 The façade of the John Brown House. Note the Palladian window above the entry.

Palladian windows appeared, doorways acquired pilasters, porticos, sidelights, and fanlights; window caps, pedimented doorways, and dormers became more common. This gradual adoption of the tastes of the homeland led to an endless variety among houses, some of which at first sight might seem very similar.

After the Revolution the Georgian style gave way to the Federal which, while incorporating many Georgian features, represented another radical departure. The work of architects like Bulfinch in Boston and McIntire in Salem turned fashion away from the smaller colonial houses and toward large four-square buildings with more austere exteriors. Many houses, such as the John Brown House and the Gardner-Pingree House, were built   13 of brick and included a minimum of exterior embellishments. The interiors, however, continued in grand style. The introduction of classical motifs through design books, and particularly through the work of Robert Adam of Scotland, inspired the first generation of American architects. The masterful carving of McIntire is equal to any work from this period.

Post-1820 the Greek and the Gothic Revivals followed hard on the heels of the Federal Period and ushered in the Victorian age of American architecture. The Roman classicism of Bulfinch gave way to the Hellenic stylings, which were endlessly adaptable. Probably the most common expression of the Greek Revival is found in the addition to older houses of pillars and porticos which evoke aspects of Greek temples. The Wilcox-Cutts House exemplifies the style in full flower, though it was later to bloom in the North country of Vermont.

The Gothic Revival gave life to what would become full-blown Victorian architecture. Peaks, gables, bargeboards, and every kind of embellishment brought about a wondrously eclectic architecture, typified in Renwick's

9, 10 Detail of a first-floor archway in the John Brown House. The high quality of the carving can also be seen on the pedimented doorway on the right. The carved pillars (*right*) of the Wilcox-Cutts House look massive when viewed from this angle.

11, 12 Detail of the exterior of Kingscote (*left*). The front reception hall at Gore Place (*right*).

Newport masterpiece Kingscote, and in Justin Morrill's country homestead. The later Victorian houses, while interesting, lack the vital originality of the early Gothic ones and tend to exhibit an ostentatious fussiness.

Presenting the houses in chronological order, as I have elected to do here, can be misleading. Although this approach shows a fairly clear stylistic development, it does not always take into account the progression of styles regionally. It is important to remember that the Northern states, particularly in those areas away from the coastline, often adopted certain styles later and clung to them longer than their more cosmopolitan neighbors.

New England is a special place to those who know it. All regions have their adherents, and there is no point in disputing claims to greater beauty, superior society, or even more handsome architecture. New England, like one of its finest folk-art forms, is a brilliant patchwork of traditions and styles. It is as fascinating for its change as it is for its continuity. This New England characteristic is represented in these houses, in the people who built them, and in the objects which filled their rooms.

This book is supposed to be fun. It is not, nor is it intended to be, a seminal work of scholarship. The ground covered has mostly been trod before and the energetic work of many people more learned than the author has been tapped to bring together the information presented here. On the other hand, I hope that the approach taken to this work has a fresh quality, and that the choices made are justifiable in terms of giving an intelligent overview of New England's development and history, and of providing a window on the lives of its people.

13 The south side of the Morey House showing the three sections of the structure.

19

14, 15 An interior view of Hunter House and (*right*) a door panel from the Florence Griswold House by Childe Hassam, entitled *Springtime Nudes*.

Fairbanks House

c.1636

DEDHAM, MASSACHUSETTS

The house Jonathan Fayerbanke built in Dedham is dark and small. Low ceilings keep a modern-sized man in constant danger of a painful rap on the forehead. The upstairs floors in the oldest part slope precariously and creak ominously, while the roof-line has acquired a slightly sway-backed appearance. But despite its somewhat unprepossessing appearance, this house is a masterpiece of preservation. Not only is it probably the oldest frame structure in North America, representing a remarkable throwback to its English ancestry, but it has also been in the same family since its construction almost 350 years ago.

Jonathan and Grace Fayerbanke (the spelling changed over the years) were originally from Yorkshire, England, where church records reveal that they were married in 1617. Why they chose to sail to America sixteen years later is unknown. They came, along with other members of the family who settled in Boston, on *The Griffin*, which landed at that city in 1633. By 1635 Jonathan had determined that the new town of Contentment would be an appropriate place to settle permanently. Within a year the settlement's name was changed to Dedham after the town in East Anglia. Jonathan's signature appears on the town charter.

The original part of the Fairbanks House has only four rooms, built on the lines of many early American colonial homes. The central chimney was of paramount importance and this one is a large and fine example. Standing on a base 8 × 10 feet it has been estimated that its construction required more than 30,000 bricks. As in most early colonial homes the rooms were built around the chimney for obvious practical reasons. The plan is a simple one, with a parlor and kitchen downstairs and two sleeping chambers above. The attic, accessible only by a simple ladder, was probably also used as a sleeping loft and children could huddle close to the chimney for warmth. This house is slightly different from many of its colonial peers in that the chimney is not exactly centered. This slight off-centering gave Grace Fayerbanke a larger kitchen than parlor and is indicative of where the family spent most of their time in the long winter months. The Fayerbankes' gate-legged table, brought with them from England, still sits in the kitchen.

Jonathan was apparently a wood-turner by trade and a man of standing in the community. He was appointed to do much of the town's surveying as early as 1638, and his success in business, as well as probably in farming,

16 The tiny stairwell of Fairbanks House. The brick wall at the left is one side of the massive chimney.

is attested by the various and quite rapid additions he made to his house. A lean-to (a form we will see a great deal of in New England's early houses) was added along the back of the house and the rear roof-line was extended downwards to create a long narrow room, which in many cases, though apparently not in this one, was designed to contain the kitchen. The east and west wings were added later. The east wing had a separate entrance and chimney with two downstairs rooms (one a large parlor) and an upstairs bedchamber. In 1648 the house was valued at the then substantial sum of £28. The family farm grew as well and when Jonathan died in 1668 he left an estate totaling £214 2s 2d.

17 Façade of the original section of Fairbanks House.

18 The kitchen of
Fairbanks House.

19–21 The gate-legged table in the kitchen (*left*) came with the Fairbanks from England. The stretchers, not surprisingly, are badly worn. (*above*) An upstairs bedroom in the final addition and (*right*) a view of the roof joinery.

Very few changes were made to the house by the next eight generations of Fairbanks who lived in it. A beehive baking oven was added in 1780 and the fireplaces were modified in the mid-nineteenth century in the interest of efficiency. The basic construction, however, was undisturbed. Parts of the interior were never even plastered, leaving the beams exposed as they were the day they were joined.

The location of the farm near the center of Dedham and declining family fortunes led eventually to the selling off of much of the property. The house is now on a small piece of land not far from Dedham's main street. Though much of the Fairbanks furniture was sold, some of it has been recovered and a number of early family pieces are on view in the house.

Ironically a bolt of lightning ended the Fairbanks' occupancy. Rachel, who had inherited the house in 1879, was asleep in the east upstairs bed-chamber when lightning struck the house and killed her dog, who was sleeping under her bed. Rachel left soon afterwards, but the family subsequently formed a foundation, which has maintained the house ever since.

Arguments will rage about what house or what portion of what house is actually the oldest frame building in America, and continued research will only add more layers of scholarly information and pose new questions. 27

Nevertheless, the importance of this ancient American house is assured. Abbott Lowell Cummings, whose fine book, *The Framed Houses of Massachusetts Bay, 1625–1725*, deals in great detail with the Fairbanks House, explains why. Because so little has been done to the house it is strikingly easy for the trained eye to observe how it reflects its English ancestry. Jonathan probably hired older carpenters to work for him and consequently the structure retains more Elizabethan characteristics than any other surviving frame house in North America. Most of this evidence is found in a detailed study of the joinery done by Cummings. He states that "The Fairbanks house . . . can be readily identified with East Anglia in all major respects of both profile and detail . . . The modular relationship of the individual units of the roof . . . is also consonant with East Anglian work of the early seventeenth century. . ."

The Fairbanks' extended occupation of the house and their instinct to preserve it has left us with an architectural and historic treasure, an open book for the architectural historian. The wattle and daub insulation and the split wide-board lathing can be examined, and the unplastered interior walls of overlapped boards are clearly visible. The stout oak frame, pegged together more than three centuries ago, still stands as a testament to those who braved the rigors of frigid winters and unknown dangers to settle here.

22,23 Rear view of Fairbanks House, clearly showing the central section and lean-to, as well as the later additon, and (*right*) the lean-to, looking through to the east wing.

Stanley-Whitman House

c.1660

FARMINGTON, CONNECTICUT

In 1640 seventeen men left Hartford, Connecticut, in search of precious open land for farming. The spot they chose, at the bend in a river, was incorporated as Farmington in 1645. In its time Farmington reigned as one of Connecticut's most important centers, eclipsing Hartford in both size and population. Gradually its vast size was cut down as various towns incorporated separately. Despite its diminished commercial position and Hartford's growth, Farmington has always maintained a special place in Connecticut history. This position is certainly what prompted Samuel Clemens, when asked by Queen Victoria where he came from, to reply, ''Nine miles from Farmington, Ma'am.'' Clemens, of course, lived in Hartford.

The Stanleys had come to Massachusetts from England in 1634. Stanley senior died during the Atlantic crossing and his son John was adopted by his uncle Thomas. They settled in New Town, Massachusetts, but soon chose to move on, because of the common complaint of lack of land. Ten years later young John Stanley married one Sarah Scott and moved to Farmington.

Farmington was typical of many interior New England farming communities in the seventeenth century. Houses were clustered around a main street with rectangular lots for farming spread out behind. The closeness of the community was critical for defensive and economic reasons, although relations with the nearby Indians were generally peaceful. A commercial bargain was struck whereby the settlers ploughed the fields and the Indians would cut wood and barter corn and hides. Hunting and fishing privileges were shared. Energetic attempts were made to convert and educate the Indians. The massacre of 1704 which devastated the frontier town of Deerfield sent shock waves through Farmington, and a number of houses were fortified as a result, but no immediate trouble ensued. There were occasional incidents over the years, the most serious usually being caused by overzealous revelry, brought about by the settlers' selling rum to the Indians. Inevitably the settlers' continuing demand for farmland drove the Tunxis Indians first north and then west, and by the late eighteenth century the tribe had almost completely dispersed.

Having spent his first fifteen years in Farmington on the main street, John Stanley determined to build a fine house on what is now High Street.

24 Façade of the Stanley-Whitman House. Note the overhang, the pendants, and the casement windows.

25, 26 The original kitchen (*left*) with the summer or load-bearing beam above, and (*above*) a view of the exterior with its classic overhang and pendants.

The house is a classic seventeenth-century-style structure (see Notes, p. 206) comprising four main rooms surrounding a massive central chimney. The downstairs rooms are notable for their very wide and deep fireplaces. In many early American houses the fireplaces were made shallower in later years, because it was determined that smaller fireplaces threw heat more efficiently, and the larger ones were no longer necessary for cooking purposes. In this case the masonry is all original, although a kitchen lean-to was added about 1760.

The lean-to changed the exterior lines of the house quite dramatically. Originally the rear roof-line would have been quite sharply pitched, but the shape was modified to accommodate the addition. The façade, however, is the most distinctive feature of the exterior. It has a classic second-story overhang with decorative pendants below the eaves. There have been many theories concerning the use of these overhangs, which were quite common on finely built seventeenth-century houses, and survive in a number of examples. The two primary explanations have been that they were built for defensive purposes or for protection from foul weather. However, the true explanation is probably that they were purely decorative, a memory of architecture which the settlers left behind in Europe.

33

This kind of decorative detail clearly indicates that this was the house of a successful Farmington gentleman.

27 The parlor fireplace.

John Stanley lived in his house until his death in 1706. The inventory and surviving records show that he left a substantial estate valued at £329, as well as a sizable amount of furniture for the time, and even a small library. The same year that John Stanley died the Farmington congregational church called a new minister, the Rev. Samuel Whitman. The church was the center for most activities in a town like Farmington, and the minister was probably the most important person in this small society. The arrangements made for Whitman are indicative of his exalted station. A house was built for him, he received his firewood, forty acres of land, and the princely sum of £100 per annum. In 1707 he married Sarah Stoddard from Northampton, Massachusetts. They had seven children.

28 This bedroom is one of the four main rooms.

The Stanley house on High Street was apparently bought for their second child Solomon when he married Susanna Cole of Farmington in 1736. (The house had had two different owners between John Stanley's death and Samuel Whitman's purchase.) Like his father, Solomon was an important figure in Farmington. He served as Town Clerk for twenty-four years, including the tumultuous years of the Revolution. Farmington was no Tory stronghold. The town provided three regiments of patriots, Rochambeau camped there twice, and Washington passed through at least six times.

The house stayed in the Whitman family for the first quarter of the nineteenth century, and then passed through various owners. It was restored in the twentieth century, and donated to the Farmington Village Green and Library Association, which maintains it as a museum.

29–31 Three views of the Stanley-Whitman House showing (*above*) details of the windows and boarding, (*left*) the old well, and (*right*) the front entry.

Wanton-Lyman-Hazard House

*c.*1700

NEWPORT, RHODE ISLAND

In August of 1765 Newport was the site of some of the most destructive activity in the New England colonies when the Stamp Act provoked violent and angry outbursts. Martin Howard Jr., an active royalist in a community where his politics had a sizable amount of support, discovered the existence of an angry opposition when he took an advertisement in *The Newport Mercury* advocating that Rhode Island be placed under the direct control of the Crown. The reaction was furious and immediate. Howard was burned in effigy, along with two of his royalist compatriots, and large crowds roamed the streets of Newport. Meanwhile, Howard had wisely taken refuge on the British warship *Cygnet*, which was in the harbor.

Though the crowd were unable to find Howard, they were determined to let him know that his departure had been noted. They funneled up Broad Street and took their anger out on his house, smashing doors, tearing out windows, breaking furniture, and stealing books and other goods. When Howard returned and viewed the destruction, he decided that a hasty retreat from Newport was the best course. Although he received restitution for damages and petitioned for the return of stolen property, he still put the house up for sale at auction. The purchaser was an influential Quaker merchant named John G. Wanton, the first of the three whose names became linked to the house.

The house that Wanton bought was an impressive structure. It was built just at the turn of the seventeenth century by Stephen Mumford and his wife Mary. They built wisely and well. The lot was a good distance from some of the marshier areas nearer the water, and close to what was then the center of Newport. It faced Broad Street which provided direct access to the harbor and wharves. The house contained four large rooms. Each room had a fireplace provided by the huge pilastered central chimney, one of the finest features of the house. The Mumfords needed the space. They were the first of several couples to raise large families in the house. Between 1698 and 1711 Mary bore Stephen eight children. Possibly as a result of this multitude a lean-to kitchen was added at some point prior to 1725, either by Mumford or by Richard Ward, to whom Mumford sold the house in 1724. The lean-to had a separate chimney and boasts a large

32, 33 Two views of the Wanton-Lyman-Hazard House.

34, 35 The ell kitchen (*left*) and fireplace (*right*) of the Wanton-Lyman-Hazard House.

fireplace and some of the original diamond-shaped wall decorations. Ward was a man of some stature. In 1741 he became Colonial Governor of Rhode Island, a position his son would later hold during the Revolution. Between 1749, when Ward sold the house, and 1757, when Martin Howard bought it, the house had two owners. The first was a tailor called Maryatt and the second was a tanner named Earl.

Following Howard's retreat from Newport and the devastation of his house John Wanton had to spend at least £60 on repairs. He then moved in his family and his business. Wanton's first wife and son had both died, but in 1760 he had married Mary Bull Nichols. They had a daughter in 1763 named Mary, who was known in Newport as "charming Polly," and three years later a son, Gideon. Wanton was a merchant and a Quaker of standing, but his most notable contribution to Newport history was probably his daughter Polly.

Polly was in her teens during the Revolution, and her charm attracted the attention of many a gentleman. The legend goes that while sitting on the front steps of her father's house she saw Major Daniel Lyman ride by, probably on his way to join Washington's army at Cambridge in 1776, and they instantly fell in love. The story is certainly difficult to substantiate, but it has been told in Newport for generations and has become part of local lore. The two had some opportunity to see each other again in the next few years as Lyman served in Newport as senior aide to Admiral de Ternay when the French fleet was stationed there. (De Ternay was living in Hunter House.) On January 20, 1782, after Polly had reached the age of eighteen, the pair were married.

During the next few years the old house faced a population explosion of mammoth proportions. The Lymans proceeded to produce thirteen children in rapid succession, and though John Wanton deeded the house to his daughter and son-in-law, he did not move out. Another addition was built on the rear of the house to accommodate the huge household, which also included servants. The addition had four more rooms, but was later torn down.

36, 37, 38 The keeping room (*left*), looking out toward Broad Street, and (*above*) the upstairs hallway. The intersticed chimney can just be seen on the right. Norman Isham considered the bedroom (*right*) above the keeping room one of the greatest seventeenth-century rooms in America; the painted paneling is quite rare.

Daniel Lyman had a distinguished and busy career. Washington appointed him Surveyor of the Port of Newport; he also built bridges, practiced law, and ended up as Chief Justice of the Supreme Court of Rhode Island. In 1808 he bought a house near Providence and, probably pressed by career considerations, moved there. The house in Newport, however, remained in the clan.

The Lymans' second daughter Harriet married an up-and-coming Newport lawyer named Benjamin Hazard, who later served as Speaker of the Rhode Island House of Representatives. Harriet and Benjamin had eight children. Two of the daughters lived out their lives in the house. The last of them died in 1911 at the age of ninety-eight. The house then stood empty for sixteen years until it was purchased by the Newport Historical Society in 1927.

Though the Wanton-Lyman-Hazard House is basically quite simple its architectural significance goes beyond its venerable age. The steep roof, for instance, with its kicked-out cornice is not a common form, and it has the uncommon effect of making the upstairs ceilings higher than those downstairs. The eminent New England architectural historian Norman Isham felt that the bedroom above the keeping room was "one of the great American seventeenth century rooms." When he restored the room he exposed the chamfered ceiling beams and the gunstock corner posts which measure twelve inches square. Of particular importance is the fireplace wall, which was crudely marbleized to imitate paneling, a very early example of this kind of decoration.

Gilman Garrison

c.1715

EXETER, NEW HAMPSHIRE

The dating of houses is a difficult matter when documentary evidence is non-existent or sketchy. Tax records are useful in that if one sees a large leap in the value of a property one can assume that some construction has probably occurred. The actual joinery of a house is also a valuable tool for the educated eye, but even this can lead to very diverse conclusions. In many cases the accepted date is the product of long-standing local tradition which can take years to break down, even in the face of over-whelming evidence. Often too much emphasis is put on protecting an early date. The ensuing debate has a tendency to obscure the features which are truly important about the building. The Gilman Garrison, for instance, is a remarkable house whether it was built in 1690 or earlier, which most historians now reject, or in 1715, which seems more likely.

The history of the Gilman family in Exeter goes a good deal further back than either of the above dates. Edward Gilman arrived in Exeter in 1647 and was granted a hundred acres of land with mill and timber rights. By 1650 Gilman and his brothers John and Moses had two saw mills in town. Edward left Exeter a few years later, probably to escape financial difficulty, and most of his assets passed to his brother John. He was more successful than Edward, and he also began a family political tradition. In 1652 he was made Selectman in Exeter, and when New Hampshire formed its first government he was chosen to serve as Councillor to the Royal Governor.

It has long been assumed that this John Gilman built Gilman Garrison, an assumption based on dating the house in the latter half of the seventeenth century. This view has been called into question in recent years, and it is now felt that the garrison was probably built around 1715. The first traceable mention is in 1719, when the house was licensed as a tavern. If this last date is accepted then it is also clear that the house was built, not by Exeter's first John Gilman, but by his son, also called John. Gilman senior died in 1708. Acceptance of the later date has almost no effect on the overall value and importance of this house.

From the exterior, the clapboarded house looks like any one might find on the main street of a New England town. It has two clearly defined sections, similar in size, which are joined to form a right angle. Even if the two sections were built at different times, there is very little to lead the casual observer to the conclusion that there is anything very special going

39 Gilman Garrison as seen from the Exeter main street.

on here. One of the two sections, however, is a log garrison house, now largely covered both inside and out. It is one of the very few log structures still standing in New England, and an important example of a type of building peculiar to the Piscataqua region of Maine and New Hampshire where defense against attack was a major preoccupation. In towns like Exeter the threat of Indian raids was still very real in the early eighteenth century. The Maine coast was virtually deserted because of attacks in the late seventeenth century, the Deerfield massacre occurred in 1704 and, as we have seen, the people of Farmington, Connecticut, who on the whole had had good relations with the Indians, garrisoned a number of their houses as a result. It is not so surprising, therefore, that a garrison house should have been built in Exeter as late as 1715.

45

40, 41 Front entrance and
landing of the Gilman
house.

42, 43 Puncheon floor room (*left*) with split-log flooring. Note, too, the summer beam and scratch-molded joists and (*right*) the dovetailed log joinery.

The log section is also of architectural significance because two major types of log house building are represented in one structure. On the first story the logs are slotted into the corner posts, while on the second story they are dovetailed together. The logs are enormous hemlocks, and in one room the floor is actually constructed of split tree-trunks. There are various places in the house where the logs are exposed. Some of the joists are scratch molded, which is unusual in log buildings and strengthens the argument that this is a later log house which incorporated certain design features of other types of contemporary houses. The fittings for a portcullis door are still visible in the garrison.

The second John Gilman turned the garrison over to his son Peter in 1732, who was living in it and keeping a shop there. Peter enjoyed a successful political career, much like his grandfather. He served in the legislature at Portsmouth almost continuously from 1735 to 1768, and was speaker from 1766 to 1768. He was an opponent of Governor Benning Wentworth, but when Wentworth's nephew John became Governor in 1771 Peter was appointed Councillor, the same post his grandfather had

44, 45 Daniel Webster's desk in the Gilman house and (*right*) the dining room.

held. He was also involved in the founding of Dartmouth College in Hanover, New Hampshire, and was a member of that institution's first board of trustees.

It was Peter who built the second section of the house, and also probably made many of the changes to the garrison. In 1772 he added the wing which is so completely different from the earlier section. Rough-hewn logs were replaced by exquisite paneling, even in the upper bedchamber, where the paneling covers all four walls. As in the Wells-Thorn House at Deerfield, the difference in the two sections is indicative of the changed status of the town and particularly, in this case, of the owner. The Council Room below the bedchamber has equally elegant paneling and a fireplace flanked by stop-fluted pilasters, It is called the Council Room because

John Wentworth's council were supposed to have used it for meetings.

After Peter Gilman's death in 1788 the house was sold to Ebenezer Clifford, an architect, carpenter, and inventor, whose impact on the town was enormous. He worked on many important buildings in the Exeter area, including the first Phillips Exeter Academy Building (1794) and the First Congregational Church (1798). As an inventor he was best known for a diving bell he developed for salvaging goods from sunken vessels. It was during Clifford's time that young Daniel Webster, then a student at the Academy, lived in a small room in the old part of the house. There are a number of etched signatures and inscriptions in panes of glass, and one of them is reputed to be Webster's.

Clifford died in 1821, but one of his daughters stayed on in the house until 1863. It was then bought by a woman named Asenath Darling, who continued Betsy Clifford's hat shop which had been established at the house. When Mrs. Darling died in 1893 she left the house to her sister Jane Hardy, who was the first truly to appreciate the house's historical significance. After her death in 1912 the house was bought by Mrs. Albertus Dudley, completing a remarkable story of feminine ownership. The Dudleys did a great deal to preserve and restore the house and when Mr. Dudley died in 1961 it was left to the Society for the Preservation of New England Antiquities.

46, 47 Stenciled floorboards (*bottom left*) are an attractive feature of the house. An upstairs bedroom in the later section gives an idea of the paneling.

48 A good example of the etched inscriptions found in a number of panes of glass in the house.

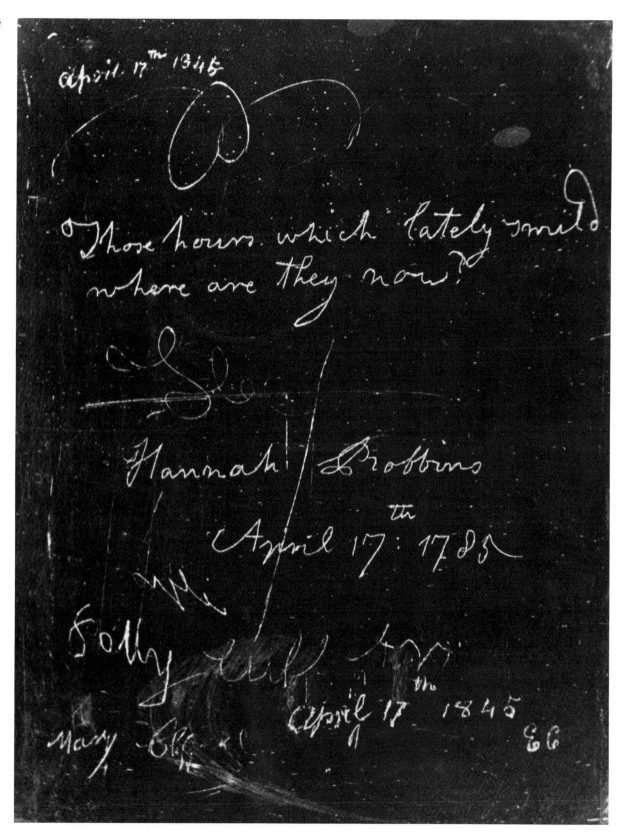

49 The Wells-Thorn
House.

Wells-Thorn House

1717-1751

DEERFIELD, MASSACHUSETTS

No frontier town in New England possesses a richer history than Deerfield. Historically, its importance lies in its long-held position as a frontier outpost. For many years it stood as the western and northernmost settlement in the Massachusetts interior, and was a critical strategic point on the Connecticut river. The town lived constantly under the threat of hostile Indian attack, often with healthy assistance from the French in Canada. Its position invited such unfortunate attention. Deerfield is also important for its remarkable state of preservation. The traditional layout of a New England town along a simple main street with the church at its center is still clearly visible and the short walk along Old Deerfield's main street is like a trip to an unchanged past.

In 1666 John Pynchon of Dedham, Massachusetts, purchased 8000 acres of land in order to reimburse people from that town whose land had been confiscated to provide space for John Eliot's Missionary Indians. It did not take long for land-hungry settlers to arrive, and lay out the village street in the classic New England pattern. The town they founded has always been known as Deerfield. The ownership of the land they occupied, however, was to be violently contested. Hostilities soon broke out with the Indians. In 1675 King Philip, the English name for Metacomet, chief of the Wampanoag tribe, waged the bloodiest of the Indian wars in New England. A loosely constructed Indian confederacy attacked frontier targets and destroyed crops. Eventually the solidarity of the settlers prevailed over the disintegration of the tribal alliance and in 1676 Metacomet was betrayed and killed. His death broke the back of Indian resistance, but Deerfield had been devastated and abandoned.

In 1677 a few settlers returned. They were quickly captured and taken to Canada, but in 1682 an even larger group arrived. This determined band built a stockade and probably garrisoned many of their houses, but their attempt to settle permanently was also doomed. On February 29, 1704, in one of the most famous Indian attacks in American history, French troops and Abenaki Indians decimated the population of Deerfield. This was as a direct result of French intervention to prevent an English treaty with the Abenaki tribe. Of the 268 inhabitants more than 50 died and 112 were taken prisoner and marched to Canada. In 1706, however, some former inhabitants returned and this time, despite sporadic difficulties, they remained.

50 Detail of a chair back.

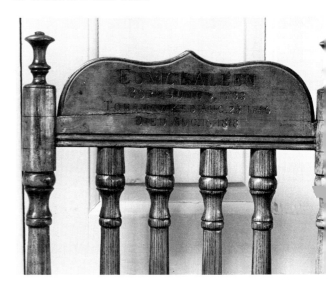

51 South side of the house, clearly showing the two main sections of the structure.

The façade of the 1751 portion of the Wells-Thorn house is far from being the most impressive of the houses on Deerfield's main street. Apart from the fine colonial blue paint which has been restored to this portion, the house has few distinguishing features. The large carved entry door, so typical of this part of the Connecticut Valley and particularly of Deerfield, was removed in the nineteenth century. The only embellishments that remain are the dentiled cornice and window caps, which were probably added during modifications in the 1780s.

Behind the unimposing façade, however, is one of the more interesting houses in Deerfield. In 1717, when the threat of Indian attack was still painfully real, Ebeneezer Wells built the first house, which is now the ell on the front portion. The structure is very simple: one chimney, two rooms, and a garrett. The dark wide boards (nearly all of them lined up horizontally because most of the walls were exterior ones) and casement windows of this tiny dwelling give it a distinctly seventeenth-century

52, 53 The gathering room (*left*) of the early portion of the Wells-Thorn House looking through to the later addition. The horizontal boards along the walls indicate that these walls were originally external ones. The Federal parlor (*right*) still has an air of distinction.

feel. The present furnishings are designed to bear this out. Wells, a farmer, soldier and tavern-keeper, became a leading citizen in Deerfield, along with his wife Abigail. An indication of his wealth is the silver tankard he left to the church on his death in 1758.

The New England tradition of a family building an addition, sometimes several, to an existing house in order to accommodate new generations is a venerable one. It is somewhat rare, however, to find the owner, especially a childless one, presiding over the building of the two major sections of his frontier home, particularly when the second came thirty-four years after the first. Whether or not Wells built the 1751 addition to house his tavern is uncertain, and it seems unlikely that he finished all of the interior at once, despite his growing wealth. It was a fairly common situation. While some might have been able to afford to build a structure, others found it necessary to leave parts of the interior unfinished until a later, more economically comfortable, time. The north parlor in this house, for instance, was probably not finished until the early nineteenth century, since the room has a distinctly Federal flavor. The south parlor, on the other hand, was probably completed by Wells himself, and might have housed his tavern.

The front of Wells' house is dramatically different from the earlier section. The ceilings are higher, the rooms larger, and the windows

54 Later front doorway on the 1851 façade. Still visible is the outline indicating where the original scrolled Connecticut Valley doorway once was.

sashed, with interior shutters. The entire effect is one of spaciousness and light as opposed to the earlier dark and cramped quarters. The difference is indicative of changes in both Deerfield and Wells. Wells' standing in the community and financially had obviously changed, but more important Deerfield's world-view was different. The tiny, almost tentative quarters of 1717, where function and protection were paramount, had been replaced by substantial housing and the confidence to seek inspiration from design books rather than from defensive strategies.

Following Wells' death the house was taken over by his nephew of the same name. He made few changes, but his son, who inherited the house in 1783, did make some alterations, including the exterior embellishments

55 Now a dining room, this room in the 1751 section of the house was finished by Wells, possibly to house his tavern.

mentioned above. Hezekiah Strong, an Amherst lawyer, bought the house in 1801, and though he only stayed for seven years, he is probably the owner who finished the north parlor and the chamber above, which he used as his office. Strong sold the house to a Deerfield shopkeeper, Orlando Ware. The Wares kept the house throughout the nineteenth century and were responsible for removing the carved entry door, which they replaced with an understated Greek Revival one. The Wares sold the house to Dr. E. C. Thorn, who made a real effort to fill the house with appropriate pieces, some of which he took in payment for outstanding doctor's bills. The house is now part of the Historic Deerfield restoration, and open to the public the year round.

Sayward House

c.1720

YORK, MAINE

In 1745 an audacious band of New England colonists launched an expedition against the ostensibly impregnable fortress of Louisbourg on Cape Breton Island, Nova Scotia. William Pepperell, a prominent Kittery merchant, was selected to lead 4000 militiamen on this seemingly impossible mission against the French fortress. (His second-in-command was Samuel Waldo, an unpopular Falmouth merchant who figures in the story of Tate House.) Pepperell's colonial crew laid siege to the fortress, assisted by a blockade provided by British ships-of-the-line, and then orchestrated an outrageous commando raid which was likened at the time to a Harvard commencement party. George II was so pleased with its success that he made Pepperell a baronet, and Pepperell, in turn, rewarded his subordinates. Jonathan Sayward of York, Maine, who had commanded the *Seaflower*, probably a troop transport, during the expedition, was presented with a brass hot-water urn in appreciation of his efforts. This urn is still prominently displayed in Sayward's house in York, and its survival is indicative of the remarkable state of preservation of this typical coastal home.

Jonathan Sayward's town of York is one of the oldest settlements in Maine. It was first established as a fur-trading outpost by the pilgrims, and was probably chosen because of its position at the foot of Mount Agamenticus, which rises by the town. The hill made for a fine landfall. Ferdinando Gorges, who made further attempts to colonize the Maine coast after obtaining the rights to it in 1639, decided that the spot would make a good place to establish his first "city." Thanks to Gorges' penchant for the grand gesture, York has the honor of being the first chartered English city in North America. It was then called Gorgeana. In 1652 the city was downgraded to a more appropriate level and became the town of York. During the late seventeenth century Indian attacks devastated the coastal settlements of Maine and towns to the north of York, such as Falmouth, were completely deserted. Settlers who were not caught or killed retreated to the safety of Massachusetts, which administered the province at the time. York was also attacked and many of its inhabitants taken captive, but at no point was the attempt to settle the spot totally abandoned. As of 1691 it was one of only four towns left inhabited on the Maine coast.

In 1720 Joseph Sayward, Jonathan's father, bought a house from one

58 A rear view of Sayward House.

Noah Peck. The house was then described as "new." Though a substantial two-story structure for its time, it is in fact a fairly simple house. Its construction was not based on pattern books, nor was it an attempt to evoke memories of faraway places. It is a practical solid dwelling, typical of the kind of house built in hardy trading towns like York in the early eighteenth century. Its straightforward style is a product of local traditions.

Joseph Sayward was an important man in York, but not a particularly successful one. He was a millwright who couldn't seem to mill correctly and he was constantly being pulled out of financial scrapes, at least once by the town itself. Jonathan's purchase of the house in 1735 for £200 was probably necessitated by impending financial disaster.

Jonathan was decidedly more successful than his father, describing himself in turn as a "trader," a "coaster," and a "marriner." The water-front location of the house proved useful, as he built his wharf directly in front and his mill right next door. He also made some changes in the house, the major improvement being the addition of interior paneling. The Sayward house and business finally matched their station. Jonathan's standing further improved when in 1758 his daughter, and only child, Sarah married into the Barrell family, an important Boston mercantile clan.

Sayward's devotion to his king may have come in part as a result of his participation in the glorious conquest of Louisbourg, but regardless of its source his Toryism was unshakeable. He was immortalized in Paul Revere's famous revolutionary broadside entitled "A Warm Place – Hell." In the broadside sixteen famous loyalists were ridiculed for their vote to rescind the "Circulatory Letter" opposing taxes levied on the colonists. Sayward is described as "His E————y's chief Soothsayer and grand Oracle of Infallibility."

This kind of notoriety did not make Sayward particularly popular in York and he was eventually stripped of all his public offices. His business suffered, and he was so afraid of being driven from the town that he carried £200 in his pocket at all times. He was, however, destined to outlive the open fury of the Revolution, and, unlike some others of his political persuasion, he elected to remain in the United States, and lived in York until his death in 1797.

The house stayed in the family throughout the nineteenth century, but unfortunately its inhabitants were plagued by another familial legacy. Jonathan Sayward's mercantile acumen proved to be something of an aberration and his grandson, Sayward Barrell, who inherited, turned out to have the business sense of his great-grandfather Joseph.

While Sayward Barrell's lack of commercial success did not leave his clan in abject poverty, it did mean that there was very little money to redesign the house or buy new furniture. This turned out to be fortunate for posterity for as the nineteenth century wore on the family developed a reverence for the articles of their own history. The comparison of an 1822 inventory with one of 1889 has shown that only a sofa, a rocking chair, and stoves had been added, while virtually nothing was removed. The famous brass urn from Louisbourg has not only been in the same house

59, 60 This landward entry would have been largely secondary during the years of Jonathan Sayward's success as a trader. The porch (*right*) was added by Elizabeth Wheeler, a direct descendant of Jonathan's, in the early 1900s.

61–64 (*left*) The back stairwell and (*right*) the parlor fireplace. (*below*) The main stairwell and a bedroom. The slant-front desk is early eighteenth century and is believed to have been built in the York area. The handsome highboy is walnut veneered and was also probably built in or around York.

since 1745, but for at least the last hundred years it has been in the same room.

The same is true of most of the furniture, which has been left in the same position for generations. Many of the pieces are exceptional, including a fine set of Portsmouth side chairs of *c.* 1760, an early eighteenth-century slant-front desk, possibly made in York, and a black walnut veneered chest of drawers from the same period, also made in the York area. Even some of the china in the parlor corner cupboard is identifiable as having been brought back from Louisbourg by Jonathan.

In 1900 the house with all its contents was purchased from the Barrells by a direct descendant of Jonathan Sayward, Elizabeth Wheeler. She chose to use the house as a summer home and added the porch which is so typical of Maine summer residences; she also painted the woodwork. Otherwise she left the house as it was. Her heirs later gave the house to the Society for the Preservation of New England Antiquities. As an illustration of the homelife of an eighteenth-century New England coastal merchant it is an irreplaceable treasure.

Ashley House

c.1730

DEERFIELD, MASSACHUSETTS

In 1726 Moses Nash sold lot Number 2 on Deerfield's main street to John Wells, a Deerfield merchant, for £70. The deed did not state the existence of any buildings on the property, and it is probable that the lot had been vacant since the massacre of 1704. John Wells was apparently quite an industrious gentleman. When he sold the property ''. . . with the edifices . . . thereon'' to Jonathan Ashley six years later the value had risen to £251. Presumably one of those edifices was the dwelling house from which Parson Ashley fought for the souls and consciences of Deerfield's residents for the next forty-seven years.

Ashley came to Deerfield almost immediately after his graduation from Yale in 1730. His formal call to serve as minister to the people of Deerfield came in 1732 when he was twenty years old. The land he bought there in 1733 served as the Ashley family homestead for the next six generations. In 1736 he married Dorothy Williams, daughter of the Reverend William Williams of Hatfield. From the very first it was clear that Parson Ashley had come to Deerfield to stay; it was also clear that he was determined to be outspoken on issues secular as well as spiritual. He seems to have had an opinion on almost everything, but some issues and controversies did more to shape Ashley's career than others.

The first dispute in which he engaged was doctrinal, and concerned the extension of church membership to all who wished it, a liberal stand which Ashley supported. Ashley's cousin and fellow preacher Jonathan Edwards rejected the Half-Way Covenant which encouraged Ashley's position. The argument raged throughout the 1740s and eventually Edwards' congregation in Northampton dismissed him. Ashley also spent many years trying to arrange for the bequest of Ephraim Williams to be used to establish a college at Deerfield. Despite tremendous effort – he even obtained the approval of the Royal Governor – his plan failed. The bequest eventually led to the founding of Williams College in Williamstown.

Ashley's greatest trial, however, was yet to come. His loyalty to the king had always been clearly articulated and as the Revolution approached he showed no inclination to change. His son Jonathan was listed, along with Jonathan Sayward of York, as one of the miscreants on Paul Revere's broadside ''A Warm Place – Hell.'' Ashley junior was also named as one of two ''Under Graduates in his E———y's political Academy for teaching passive Obediance and Non-Resistance." Father and son, who were similar in many ways, both saw the Revolution as a civil struggle inspired by traitorous and Godless men. Ashley held his ground. In June of 1780 a council was called to discuss his dismissal, but it disbanded without reaching a decision. Before another meeting could be called Ashley died, on August 28, 1780.

The Ashley family continued to inhabit their corner of the Deerfield street. Jonathan's son Elihu was the next occupant. He was a doctor and one of the most interesting members of the clan. The next generations gradually turned to farming. In 1869 Jonathan Ashley's great-grandson John determined that the family home was not adequate. Rather than tearing the old house down he pulled it back from the street and turned it into a tobacco shed. It remained there, boarded up and virtually gutted, until 1945.

The story of the reconstruction of Ashley House is not only central to the story of Old Deerfield, but it is also a benchmark in the history of the preservation movement in America. When the project was first mooted the house was little more than a shell, albeit a fairly sturdy one. The sills were rotten, the windows boarded up, and a tree had grown up in front of the main entrance once adorned by a fine scroll-carved Connecticut Valley doorway. The only tangible signs of the old house's former stature were some remnants of paneling inside.

Through the efforts of Mr. and Mrs. Frank Boyden (he was then head-master of Deerfield Academy) and Mr. and Mrs. Henry Flynt, Americana collectors with an intense interest in the Academy and in Deerfield, the old house was returned to its former location. (The 1869 house had been purchased by the Academy and moved down the street to the campus.)

The actual relocation of the building was only the beginning of a seem-ingly impossible task. The inch-by-inch reconstruction required pains-taking detective work. It was determined that there had been a lean-to on the back of the house at the north side, and that the house had originally had a pitched roof, which was converted to a gambrel one at a later date, probably during Jonathan Ashley's lifetime. The prior existence of a classic Deerfield doorway was confirmed by the configuration of the clapboards around the entrance.

The interior presented special problems. Every scrap of remaining wall-paper had to be saved, every chip of plaster examined, every speck of paint analyzed, and every mortice investigated to determine where interior walls met exterior ones. Ceiling joists, the configuration of the attic rafters, and brick debris made it clear where the chimneys had been. It was confirmed that Elihu Ashley had added an ell onto the house, probably about 1787, which housed his kitchen. The lean-to, originally the kitchen, was converted into a bedroom at that time. Both the lean-to and the ell were apparently lost when the house was moved in 1869 and they had to be completely reconstructed.

Every conceivable shred of evidence was used. Ashley's records of expenditures were scrutinized to try to establish when he made what

66 Ashley House.

repairs and changes. George Sheldon's nineteenth-century *History of Deerfield* contained a number of descriptions of the interior of the house and these were incorporated in the reconstruction plans.

To say that the finished product, which was completed in 1948, is remarkable is a masterpiece of understatement. Obviously there are two ways to look at this house within the context of this book. The first is to point out that very little here, other than the frame itself and some pieces of family furniture which have been restored to the house, is original. The second is to stress the importance of the reconstruction. The house, while of major historical importance, stands as a symbol of the American preservation movement. It was also the inspiration for the continued preservation of Old Deerfield, which is without a doubt one of the most influential of such projects in America. Somehow the indisputable fact that it *is* a reconstruction pales in comparison with this accomplishment.

73

67, 68 The kitchen in the reconstructed lean-to
as it was during Jonathan Ashley's tenancy and
(*below*) the parlor.

69–71 These interior views give little hint
of the painstaking detective work behind the
reconstruction of Ashley house.

Adams Mansion

c.1748

QUINCY, MASSACHUSETTS

Since one of the aims of this book is to examine houses that in some way tell a chapter of New England history, then the Adams Mansion in Quincy certainly deserves to be included. The Adams family's influence on New England and on American history has been second to none, and this house served as their full-time or summer residence from the time John Adams bought the house in 1787 until 1927.

"The Old House," as the family came to call it, was built just after 1730 by Leonard Vassal, a sugar planter from Jamaica. Though the farm's legal ownership was questioned during the Revolution, Vassal's daughter managed to retain title, and sold the farm to her son. He in turn sold the property to John Adams, who had had his eye on the house for quite some time.

When Adams bought the homestead in Quincy he was in England, serving as the Ambassador to the Court of St. James, but all indications suggest that he and Abigail were happy about the purchase at the time. It is important to remember that although this remarkable couple gave birth to a remarkable line they were not members of the American aristocracy. John came from four generations of New England farmers and millers in Braintree and Abigail was a minister's daughter from Weymouth. While in Europe, however, their tastes changed. They were constantly exposed to the glitter of European society, and when they returned to Quincy in 1780 they may have found their gambrel roofed "mansion" somewhat lacking. The entire house consisted of a paneled dining room and parlor downstairs, two bedrooms above and some attic rooms. The kitchen was originally separate from the house, but was attached in the late 1780s.

Abigail's disappointment in her new surroundings is quite well documented. She enjoyed the farm and approached its growth and maintenance with gusto, but was most distressed with the house, referring to it as a "wren's house." The downstairs was hopelessly small for the parties and receptions she intended to give as the wife of the first Vice-President of the United States, but she managed.

In 1800, during John's presidency, Abigail was finally able to add to the house. She built a large drawing room on the first floor so that the former drawing room became an adequate dining room. On the second floor above the new drawing room she built a study to house her husband's

72, 73 (*below*) John Adams' study, built for him by Abigail over her drawing room. (*right*) A desk fits snugly into the corner of one of the two original receiving rooms, which served at various times as a parlor and a dining room. The fine dark paneling was installed by Leonard Vassal.

burgeoning library. Books have always been an Adams family passion, whether reading, collecting or writing them. By the time of John's death the house was already filled with them and John Quincy was busily acquiring more. In 1870 his son Charles Francis Adams was forced to build a separate library to house the 15,000 volumes. Even so the house still bulges with books.

After his difficult one-term presidency John Adams returned to his newly enlarged home. On July 4, 1826, the fiftieth anniversary of the signing of the Declaration of Independence, he died sitting in the study that Abigail had made for him. Adams' political adversary and close friend Thomas Jefferson died at Monticello on the same day.

John Quincy Adams took over the house, but never spent as much time in it as his father. He made few changes, contenting himself with planting some trees and adding a passageway behind the 1730 portion of the house that connected with Abigail's addition. Apart from these improvements

74 The front of the Adams Mansion. The wing added by Abigail is at the right.

75 The Adams Mansion with the library to the left.

he left the house alone. He enjoyed the farm, but his devotion was entirely to the mechanics of politics. After completing his own single term as President in 1828 he returned to Quincy, but could not settle. He said that the house was never entirely comfortable for him after his father's death, and he was still politically restless. In 1831 he became the only man ever to return to Congress following a stint in the presidency. He was elected to the House of Representatives and served there until his death in 1848. He died at his desk in the House chamber. The desk is now in the family library at Quincy.

Charles Francis Adams, John Quincy's oldest son, inherited the house. Largely for financial reasons he seriously considered selling or leveling it. Charles Francis's career may have been somewhat less distinguished than his father's or grandfather's, but he did bring something to the family that they had lacked in past generations – money. He achieved this by being a better businessman than his predecessors and by marrying well.

76, 77 View through the upstairs bedchambers in the older part of the house and (*right*) one of the original upstairs bedrooms. Note the fine slipper chair in front of the right-hand window.

His financial position allowed him to elevate the farm to the "country seat" level to which it had always aspired. He built the famous library, and added a servants' wing – five servants were on the staff when he was in residence. He was abroad a good deal; during the critical years of the Civil War he served, like his father and grandfather, as minister to England.

Charles Francis's children were the last generation of Adams to live in the house. After his death in 1886 the family still continued to come and go. His three sons, Charles Francis Jr., Henry, and Brooks, all used the house as a retreat for writing and research. Brooks, the youngest son, was given custody of the farm and did a great deal to plan for its preservation. In 1927 the house was put in the hands of the Adams Memorial Society, which then gave it to the National Park Service, which still administers it. 83

Hunter House

c.1748

NEWPORT, RHODE ISLAND

The very mention of Newport, Rhode Island, conjures up images of great wealth, yachting, and of the massive "cottages" built by its nineteenth-century summer residents. These images, though far from a complete picture, are certainly applicable to Newport post-1830. Before the Revolution, however, Newport was a commercial center rivaling New York and Boston in trade and business. Quaker merchants thrived on the "triangular trade" of rum, slaves and molasses.

Newport's deep harbor played a large role in its prosperity. Miles of shoreline were available to ocean-going vessels, and Newport's merchants could build their wharves right in front of their grand mansion houses. These houses still line Easton's Point in Newport. Behind them are preserved many of the homes of other merchants and artisans of colonial times, such as the Townsends and the Goddards, fine furniture builders whose success was made possible by the importation of shiploads of mahogany to Newport's harbor. Preeminent among these shoreline houses is Hunter House. Despite its comparatively diminutive structure it is possibly Newport's greatest mansion; it is certainly one of the ten great colonial houses in America.

On April 12, 1748, Jonathan Nichols, a thirty-five-year-old Newport merchant and head of a thriving shipping business, purchased the lots on which Hunter House was built. Nichols was already a prominent political figure. He served in both the upper and lower Houses of the colonial legislature and ended his days as deputy governor, the same high office his father had attained.

Nichols not only built the largest portion of what we now know as Hunter House, but he also constructed a wharf and extensive warehouses. When he died in 1756 he left a massive estate which included the property at Easton's Point, a large farm in Portsmouth, Rhode Island, two ships and a half interest in a third, and seven slaves who had served his household. The total value was about £50,000. Nichols was generous with his great wealth and it was during his time at Hunter House that it acquired its title "the mansion of hospitality." Nichols' executors sold the house and outbuildings at auction to Colonel Joseph Wanton, Jr., whose grandfather, great-uncle, and father were all colonial governors. Wanton expanded the house and gave it the basic form it retains today.

Wanton was a rather flamboyant character, given to wearing lace

80 Hunter House. The handsome doorway was originally on the seaward side of the house.

finery. While at Harvard he was fined for gambling and rowdiness. His powerful connections in Newport ensured that Hunter House remained a centerpiece of Newport society. Wanton's successful business dealings included privateering and other occasionally shady transactions. Politically his life was to prove quite complicated, because he was an energetic and outspoken loyalist.

The house as Wanton completed it was magnificent, and the era of his occupation is the one that is chiefly represented in the house in its present restored state. The frame was made of heavy mortised and tenoned lumber and the house insulated with brick. Exterior detailing disguises the bulkiness of the frame construction. The most famous of these details is the front doorway framed by pilasters with scrolled broken pediment above; the pineapple over the doorway is the symbol of hospitality. The ornate entry now faces the street, but originally it was on the other side of the house overlooking the waterfront. It is important to remember that Hunter House was the center of a bustling place of business. During Newport's golden mercantile age the house stood right at the water's edge and from the office, then in the front of the house, one could watch all the activities on the wharf and in the warehouses. The lawn behind the house is mostly the result of land filling in the nineteenth century.

The promise of interior detail held out by the entry is very definitely fulfilled. The northeast parlor, for instance, has fine paneling, marbleized Corinthian pilasters, and the fireplace is flanked by shell-carved cupboards

81–83 (*left*) Hunter House from the water. The Walnut Parlor (*right*), so-called because of the fine paneling, grained to imitate walnut, and the northeast parlor (*below*) with its marbleized pillars and carved angel heads.

with carved angel heads floating above the upper corners. This display of fine detail was a symbol of great station in a colonial trading town like Newport. The paneling throughout the house is superb. Some of it was grained to imitate more expensive woods, like the furniture in the southeast parlor which was grained to simulate walnut. The furniture throughout the house has been gathered to recreate the atmosphere of the Revolutionary period and there are a number of good examples of Townsend-Goddard craftsmanship.

During the years of the Revolution Joseph Wanton's Tory position kept him on a precarious perch. His father was ousted as colonial governor by the rebels in June of 1775, and Joseph was arrested and detained at Providence in 1775 and again in 1776. He steadfastly refused to recant. Under the British occupation Wanton enjoyed his final halcyon days in the town of his birth, but when the British evacuated the city Wanton went with them to New York where he died in 1780. After his departure the State of Rhode Island confiscated the house, and with the arrival of the French fleet in the summer of 1780 they turned over the mansion to the ailing Admiral de Ternay. De Ternay died in December, but the house continued to serve as quarters for ranking French officers for most of the next year.

Following the Revolution Newport was like a ghost town, and Hunter House remained largely silent until 1805 when William Hunter, a New-

84, 85 (*left*) Detail of marbleized pilaster and angel's head in the northeast parlor, and (*above*) another view of the parlor.

86 An upstairs bedroom, looking through to the nursery.

port native and a lawyer, bought it at auction for the paltry sum of $5000. Political activity often kept Hunter away from Newport; he served in the General Assembly from 1799 to 1811, in the U.S. Senate from 1811 to 1821, and in the State Legislature from 1823 to 1825.

During the 1820s and early 1830s the Hunters lived in the house, but William was apparently not as good at making money as he was at making speeches, because the family was invariably in some financial straits. Consequently very few changes were made to the house. Possibly Hunter's greatest contribution to the house is the painting he commissioned of the family dogs. It was painted by Gilbert Stuart when the artist was thirteen and now hangs in the southeast parlor.

Between 1834 and 1844 Hunter served as American chargé d'affaires in Brazil, and during his long absences the house began to fall apart. Following his death in 1849 and his wife's in 1851, the house passed through a number of owners, and was used for a variety of purposes, from a summer house to a convent, and further damage was done, often in the interests of modernization.

In 1945 a group of concerned Newport residents banded together to purchase and restore the house. A year later the Preservation Society of Newport County was formed to oversee the restoration, and Hunter House became the cornerstone, much like Ashley House in Deerfield, of Newport's massive preservation efforts.

87 The elegant paneled dining room at Hunter
House, looking through to the office.

88 Washington's bedroom at Webb House, with
the wallpaper installed for his visit.

Webb House

1752

WETHERSFIELD, CONNECTICUT

From May 19 to May 24, 1781, George Washington stayed in Wethersfield, Connecticut, and enjoyed the hospitality of Joseph Webb, a gentleman known as one of the more gracious hosts in New England. There had been many a visitor and many a gathering at Webb's house, but this was different. An entire upstairs bedroom had been re-done just to accommodate the General during the visit. Webb had known that Washington was coming, and that his home would be used for a carefully orchestrated summit between Washington and Comte de Rochambeau, commander of the French army at Newport. Wethersfield was selected because it was almost equidistant between Newport and Newburgh, where Washington was headquartered.

At the time of the meeting Wethersfield was one of the most important towns in Connecticut, and, despite its location inland on the Connecticut River, a busy trading center. This was largely because of its deep cove harbor, which allowed fairly large ships to come up the river and dock. Probably the first ship ever built in Connecticut was not built on the coast but inland at Wethersfield; the *Tryall* was constructed there in 1649. Shipbuilding remained an important part of the town's economy until after the Revolution. The farmers in the valley used Wethersfield as the export center for their produce, and by the middle of the eighteenth century all manner of luxuries were available in town, including fine fabrics, ceramics and glass, books, and toys. One of Rochambeau's aides referred to the town as "a charming spot. ... It would be impossible to find prettier houses and a more beautiful view. I went up into the steeple of the church and saw the richest country I had yet to see in America. From this spot you can see for fifty miles around." Wethersfield was therefore an appropriate spot to hold such an historic meeting as the one between Washington and Rochambeau.

Webb House was built in 1752 by Joseph Webb Sr., a successful Wethersfield shopkeeper and West Indies merchant. When Webb died in 1761 his wife Mehitabel called for the assistance of a lawyer named Silas Deane, whom she later married. Deane became one of the more intriguing figures in the Revolution, for it was he who first went to France and enlisted the assistance of Lafayette and Von Steuben. Deane was later accused of writing treasonous letters suggesting peace without independence. Following the publication of the letters in New York Deane

89 The meeting room.

90, 91 Webb House. (*below*) The brilliantly painted shell-carved cupboard in the corner of the parlor.

remained in France. In 1789 he decided to return to America to clear his name. He died, somewhat mysteriously, on the voyage home.

The paramount issue at the conference was whether cooperation between the French and American forces was possible. Personalities were part of the problem. There is a long-standing legend that Rochambeau and Washington were perfectly matched and great friends. The historian James Thomas Flexner, among others, disputes this. He maintains that the creation of this impression was a real Revolutionary public relations coup. Whenever the two gentlemen were seen in public together they behaved animatedly and amicably, but behind the scenes this relationship was strained, tense, and mildly Machiavellian. By the time of the conference – Rochambeau and Washington had met once before at Hartford – the relationship was ripe with distrust, and Rochambeau was even rancorous. Major General Chastellux, an aide to Rochambeau and friend of Washington and Jefferson, said his superior's performance displayed "all the ungraciousness and all the unpleasantness possible."

Another point at issue was the strategic disposition of existing forces, and, needless to say, the two men differed. Rochambeau favored a move south to attack Cornwallis in Virginia, while Washington favored an attack on New York. The result of the final move on Virginia was the Yorktown campaign and Cornwallis' surrender, but there is more here than meets the eye. First of all, the resolve of the conference was not to

92 The parlor with its shell-carved cupboard at the left.

93 The rear of Webb House. The porch is a nineteenth-century addition.

move on Virginia, but to attack New York. Rochambeau was dissembling. He had indicated that he would go to New York when he had every intention of moving farther south, and he had also failed to inform Washington that a French fleet was headed north from the Indies, which Rochambeau hoped would rendezvous with the Newport fleet off Virginia. Rochambeau probably went so far as to orchestrate that fleet's refusal to assist in the New York operation, so as to leave Washington no choice but to move on Virginia.

The house where these two gentlemen locked horns over the strategic issue that would shape the end of the Revolution is a handsome gambrel-roofed structure. There is a tradition that part of the ell is actually seventeenth century, but there can be no doubt about the date of the main part of the house. The interior detailing is of the highest quality and the restoration is excellent. A conscious attempt has been made to evoke the feeling of the house at the time of Washington's visit. Much of the painted

94, 95 The attic of the ell, showing the construction of a gambrel roof. (*right*) The stairway with its finely turned newel post.

paneling has been spectographically analyzed in order to match colonial colors. These are particularly fine in the north parlor where the colors of the shell-carved cupboard are brilliantly restored. The Council Room where Rochambeau and Washington met is a re-creation of what the room might have looked like. The bedroom which Washington used still has the same wallpaper which Joseph Webb ordered for his visit, and which was put up just a few days before the Generals arrived. The attic gives a very fine view of the construction of a gambrel roof.

The house remained in the Webb family until 1802, and then, following a quick succession of owners, it passed into the hands of the Wells family in 1821. In 1915 Wells' descendants sold the house to Wallace Nutting, the famous New England photographer. During his four years there he made some changes and carried out some restoration. In 1919 the house was acquired by the Colonial Dames who maintain it, along with the Deane House and one other, as a museum.

Tate House

1755

PORTLAND, MAINE

In the 1730s the tiny settlement of Falmouth (Portland) on the coast of what is now Maine suddenly took on vital new importance. While towns farther south on the New England coast such as Portsmouth, New Hampshire, had grown dramatically, Falmouth had remained a frontier outpost. One of the sources of Portsmouth's growth was New Hampshire's forest land which yielded tall pines to supply masts for the Royal Navy. As early as 1691 The Massachusetts Charter reserved all pine of size for the King's ships. As New Hampshire's trees were plundered, the trackless virgin forest of Maine, then a territory administered by The Massachusetts Bay Colony, loomed tall and inviting.

The mast trade in Falmouth was developed by Thomas Westbrook, who served as the on-site mast agent for Samuel Waldo, a Bostonian who apparently actually held the licence. Westbrook was industrious and enormously popular in Falmouth. He built mills and the mast center at the mouth of the Stroudwater River, known as Stroudwater Landing. Waldo and Westbrook, however, had a savage falling out in the 1730s from which Waldo emerged as both victor and villain. Westbrook died in poverty in 1744.

When Captain George Tate Sr. arrived to settle at Stroudwater Landing in 1751, he was certainly an atypical New England pioneer. He was neither seeking his fortune nor his religious freedom and he was most certainly not escaping the law. He was, in fact, an established and successful businessman who had amassed a small fortune in various endeavors, including the Baltic mast trade. He was also fifty-one years of age, a venerable vintage for an eighteenth-century world traveler.

Although it is not recorded whether Tate took up the official job of mast agent immediately, it is clear that Waldo was not much in evidence in Falmouth. By 1757, two years before Waldo's death, Tate had secured the job in fact as well as effect. Almost immediately he became Stroudwater's most prominent and successful merchant.

On his arrival Tate had built a structure to house his family which was probably similar to the simple even rude dwellings built at Falmouth until that point. Even Westbrook's house had been a fairly crude half-garrison. In 1755 Tate chose to build a house which he felt befitted his station in society and also reflected his previous lifestyle in London.

The site he chose was the most prominent knoll in Stroudwater. Though

96 Tate House. Note the fine doorway and the clerestory on the third floor.

97, 98 Detail of the exterior construction of the clerestory and (*right*) the attic hallway. The rooms at the left look out through the clerestory.

the house now looks small and simple, by frontier colonial standards it is a true Georgian masterpiece. The exterior is notable for a number of features. Firstly, the number of windows is remarkable. Glass was incredibly expensive, but Tate had twelve windows on the façade and the first-floor windows had eighteen panes each. The thirteenth window on the façade is the fanlight which sits over a large pilaster-framed door with a triangular pediment. This kind of detail was previously unheard of in Falmouth and the fanlight is probably the oldest in Portland.

The most striking feature of the exterior, however, is the ''indented gambrel roof'' or ''clerestory'' which forms the front windowed wall of the three small rooms on the third floor. This style, apparently peculiar to Maine, is known in only one other example. Tate undoubtedly oversaw this design and probably liked it because it made the façade seem more impressive. These roof windows also made the small upstairs rooms far more hospitable, as well as providing a clear view of the landing. The clerestory is not repeated at the rear, and the back of the house is very plain when compared to the façade.

Tate House is built around a large central chimney and has eight fire-places in its three stories. The interior is truly the creation of a gentleman recently removed from the refinements of London society to the harsh

realities of colonial life. Every attempt is made to recreate the genteel charm of a Georgian townhouse. The downstairs parlor and dining room are elegantly paneled and the parlor includes a fine shell-carved corner cupboard. The upper moldings are embellished with narrow black painted lines, a refinement common in English townhouses of the period.

The entry hall sets the tone for the entire house. Painted floors are a New England tradition, but the hall floor is particularly fine. It is painted in a black and white diamond pattern to simulate marble, obviously unavailable in Falmouth. The stairway rises in three runs, with beautifully turned balusters and a subtly carved handrail. The curves in the handrail are matched by the wainscoting on the stairwell wall. The coffered ceiling above the stairwell is embellished in the same way as the downstairs gathering rooms.

Both the dining room and the parlor have doors leading to the large kitchen, and the kitchen and dining room have access to the ell where the back door to the house is located. The upstairs bedchambers, while not as grandly finished as the downstair rooms, are nevertheless interesting. The two main bedchambers are paneled. Such upstairs detail

99 The parlor. The ceiling trim, carving and paneling are all worthy of note.

was rare even in houses in places far more civilized than Falmouth. The third floor contains the three small rooms lighted by the clerestory. These were probably used for slaves, servants or children. The hallway off these three rooms gives one an excellent opportunity to examine the mortise and tenon and pegged construction of the house.

The use of outsize boards, which exceeded the king's legal limit in width, is indicative of Tate's standing in the community. Only a successful mast agent would have dared be so brazen. Tate lived on to the age of ninety-four, and though his first twenty years at Stroudwater were successful, the Revolution and changing business emphases in the latter quarter of the century caused the family's fortunes to flag.

The house also brought Captain Tate a most bizarre tragedy. In 1770, believing that they were in danger of being robbed, Tate's son William rigged a trap on the ell door designed, by triggering a gun, to stop and wound the thief. Tate's wife, Mary, not knowing that the trap was set at the time and exasperated with her maid who refused to brave the door, opened it and was killed. In a strange courtroom drama William was tried, convicted, and then received a King's pardon.

100 The dining room, looking through to the kitchen. The decorative painted embellishments to the ceiling molding were designed to evoke memories of London townhouses of the period.

101 The stairwell at Tate House.

106

John Paul Jones House

1758

PORTSMOUTH, NEW HAMPSHIRE

On August 12, 1781, the Chevalier John Paul Jones, recently so created by the French in recognition of his triumph over the *Serapis*, set off from Philadelphia on a circuitous route to Portsmouth, New Hampshire. The journey took him nineteen days, largely because he had to loop around New York, which the British still held. He was on his way to take command of the *America*, the first American ship-of-the-line, which had been under construction in Portsmouth since 1777. He stopped along the route to visit Robert Morris, Washington, and Rochambeau in White Plains. Morris, the financier of the Revolution, was Jones's greatest supporter and was largely responsible for securing his new command.

The Chevalier's reception in Portsmouth was regal and he found the surroundings pleasant. This was fortunate, because he was destined to spend the next year there completing and fitting out his ship. This was not his first stay in Portsmouth. He had been there in 1777 to oversee the outfitting of his then new command, *Ranger*. He renewed his acquaintance with friends such as Colonel Wendell and General Whipple and resumed what had been a somewhat stormy relationship with Colonel John Langdon. It is not certain where Jones stayed during his first visit to Portsmouth, but during his second stay he established residency at the house of Mrs. Gregory Purcell, a widow who took in boarders, and her lovely gambrel-roofed Georgian house has long since taken on the name of her most famous tenant.

Captain Gregory Purcell, who built the Jones House, was, by all accounts, a successful young Irishman who, besides being a seaman, had various business interests in and around Portsmouth. He must have been fairly well-heeled because he sought and received the approval of the Wentworth family when he married Governor Benning Wentworth's niece Sarah. By the 1750s he had prospered to the point where he was able to purchase a piece of pasture land at the corner of what is now Middle and State streets. Tax records indicate that he built his house in 1758. His financial dealings have been difficult to trace, but it is known that he owned a store on the Long Wharf in Portsmouth and was selling coal in 1760. He was also listed in 1772 as President of the "Charitable Irish Society." When he died in 1776, however, he left Sarah in rather precarious financial shape, possibly because his business skills were not as pronounced as the sketchy evidence we have suggests, or, more likely, because he also

103, 104 John Paul Jones House. The main façade and a corner of the garden.

105 This fine Georgian window looks out from the landing of the John Paul Jones House.

left an enormous brood of children. Even taking in boarders proved to be only a temporary solution. Within a decade creditors' demands had led Sarah to virtual financial ruin.

Fortunately, John Paul Jones paid his rent. During the completion of the *America* he was charged $10.00 a week. He stayed for fifty-five weeks, so he must have found the accommodation satisfactory. He was given the front bedroom over the dining room. At some point during his stay he etched his name in a pane of glass in this room, but this has now been lost.

One of the virtues of Purcell's house is how little it has changed. It was continuously inhabited until 1919 when it was purchased by the Portsmouth Historical Society, which has overseen its preservation ever since. The house makes an interesting comparison with two other coastal merchants houses discussed earlier, Tate House and Hunter House. Unlike Tate House, Purcell's house was built on a fairly grand scale, with an impressive sweeping entry, a handsome wide staircase rising in two runs, and a spacious landing graced by a tall classical Georgian window. Tate's entry hall, though magnificent for its detail, is cramped, with a small stairway running up alongside a traditional central chimney. Purcell's house is far more reminiscent of the final configuration of the entry at Hunter House, though it must be remembered that the stairway at Hunter

106, 107 The dining room and (*right*) the parlor.

House was added sometime later, albeit from a contemporary structure.

Like these other two houses Purcell's house was built with great attention to detail. The carving and paneling throughout are very fine. The simply paneled wainscoting, often broken by finely carved pilasters, and the embrasure of the window at the landing of the main stairwell are good examples. The handsome balusters on the stairwell were apparently the work of local shipwrights.

Jones's sojourn with Sarah Purcell may have been pleasant, but the denouement of his work in Portsmouth was shattering. When he arrived the construction of *America* was at a standstill, and Jones almost willed the ship toward completion. Colonel Langdon, who was supposed to finance the project, was extremely slow about producing any real money. Although Jones managed to get some assistance from his friend Robert Morris, he ended up paying for large portions of the construction himself. These problems, however, proved to be the least of his worries.

On August 9, 1782, a French ship-of-the-line went aground in the outer anchorage of Boston harbor and later sank. Congress, tired of the financial drain *America* was causing and probably also tired of Jones's haggling with Langdon, voted on September 3 to give the ship, still in the stocks at the time, to France.

At Morris's request Jones remained in command until *America*, the largest ship ever built at Portsmouth, was finally launched on November 5. Jones stated that there was so much work left to be done on the ship that it was a bit like giving a friend an "empty Egg-shell." On November 7 he left Portsmouth with his career in the U.S. Navy basically over. In 1788 he entered the Russian service and served against Turkey. He died in France in 1792. His name, however, will be tied forever to Gregory Purcell's mansion house.

109, 110 Purcell's office at the John Paul Jones
House and (*right*) the impressive entry hall.

Tapping Reeve House

1773

LITCHFIELD, CONNECTICUT

Litchfield is without question one of the most beautiful towns in New England. Its main thoroughfares are lined with magnificent eighteenth and nineteenth-century houses, all perfectly presented. It is the quintessential bucolic Connecticut village. This restful appearance belies a more energetic past, when Litchfield was one of the most important towns in Western Connecticut, a central stopping place on the coach routes which branched north to Albany, east to Boston and south to Hartford and New York. What an active place it must have been when Lyman Beecher and his children, Henry Ward, Catherine, and Harriet, lived in the rectory, Aaron Burr was a student and frequent visitor, and the politically powerful Wolcotts lived across the street from Reeve's Litchfield Law School. Ironically Tapping Reeve, who brought the Beechers to Litchfield and was at the hub of many activities in this bustling community, is probably the least known of his famous contemporaries.

Reeve was born on Long Island in 1744 and graduated from Princeton (College of New Jersey) in 1763. He remained there for seven years teaching at the Grammar School connected with the College. It was during this period that he first had contact with the Burr siblings, Aaron and Sally, who were students of Reeve's and whose father was President of the College. In 1771 he moved to Hartford and took up law in the office of Judge Jesse Root. In 1772 Reeve married Sally Burr and together they moved to Litchfield. The next year they built their house.

If the law as passed from England to its North American colonies has ever seen a more active era than the formative years of the last quarter of the eighteenth century, one would be hard pressed to find it. These few years produced the Declaration, the Articles of Confederation, the Constitution and the Bill of Rights, as well as structuring an entirely new government and judicial system. And yet the way the colonies and the new nation produced its legal practitioners was, while not exactly haphazard, at least a little relaxed. The great American law schools were not established until well after this seminal period: Transylvania (1799), Harvard (1817), Yale (1824) and Virginia (1826). Prior to the establishment of these schools lawyers were mainly trained by apprenticeship, the quality of the education largely being determined by the ability of the teacher and the time available from him. There were also a few professors who specialized in law as part of a broader curriculum at

111 Tapping Reeve House. The small wing is the 1780 addition.

112, 113 Tapping Reeve's classroom and (*above*)
Tapping Reeve House.

institutions such as William and Mary, which was the first to organize such
a program in 1779. During this critical period, however, there was only
one true law school in the United States. This school produced such
luminaries as Aaron Burr, Oliver Wolcott Jr., John C. Calhoun, Horace
Mann, Henry Baldwin, and Levi Woodbury. Its student body produced
two vice-presidents, three Supreme Court Justices, six governors of
Connecticut, four governors of other States, seventeen Senators, and
seven Foreign Ministers. This was all accomplished at the tiny law school
that Tapping Reeve ran at his home in Litchfield, Connecticut.

Reeve's house is actually one of Litchfield's simplest. The original
block has two stories with a total of six rooms and an attic. The attic was
ventilated and the hipped roof made it a perfectly adequate sleeping loft.

114 The attic, clearly showing the joinery of a hipped roof.

(The condition of the attic and the exposed beams provide a fine opportunity to observe the structure of a hipped roof.) The downstairs went through a number of different incarnations, with the parlor, for instance, sometimes serving as a classroom. It is presently set up as such. In 1780 Reeve added a downstairs wing for Sally who was very frail and found climbing stairs difficult. A formal dining room and other Victorian embellishments were later added to the rear of the house, but the core of the structure was changed very little and has been restored, as has some of the fine wall stenciling. In 1930 a group of prominent American lawyers, including Chief Justice William Howard Taft, bought the house and donated it to the Litchfield Historical Society, which has opened it to the public.

Almost immediately after his arrival in Litchfield Tapping Reeve established himself in a fairly competitive legal environment and his practice flourished. He then opened his house to law students, the first of whom was Aaron Burr. The flow of students came until his retirement in 1820 and then continued under the tutelage of James Gould, a student of Reeve's who stayed to teach and ran the school from 1820 until 1833.

Reeve was, by most accounts, one of the most charming men of his generation. Lyman Beecher spoke glowingly of him in his *Autobiography*:

> He had a pair of soft dark eyes of rare beauty, a beaming expression of intelligence and benevolence, while his soft gray hair fell in tresses to his shoulders ... His figure was tall and portly, and his manners gentle and dignified. His voice was singular, having failed for some unknown cause, so that he always spoke in a whisper, and yet so distinctly that a hundred students at once could take notes as he delivered his law lectures.

115 Aaron Burr's bedroom.

Reeve was certainly a charismatic teacher, whose vision of the law was based on a strict moral code coupled with a passionate belief in equality. In 1783 he successfully defended, with Thomas Sedgwick, Elizabeth Freeman's contention that though born a slave she deserved her freedom on the basis of the Constitution of Connecticut's claim that "All men were born free and equal." He saw the law as a tool to win the hearts and minds of people. A statement made late in his life has often been interpreted as cynical, but one suspects that when Reeve defined the law as ". . . whatever is confidently asserted and plausibly maintained," he meant that the law must be given life by those who know it, made to flex when it is appropriate and remain rigid when necessary.

James Gould, Reeve's partner from 1798 on, was a different kind of man. He provided the balance to Reeve's restless energy. Gould was a much abler administrator, a firm lawyer and teacher, and without his assistance and guidance the school would probably have closed long before declining enrolment and competition from established universities made closing inevitable. Without Reeve's vision, however, the Litchfield Law School would never have opened at all.

The law school lasted sixty years and during those years graduated 1100 students. The Tapping Reeve House sat in the center of an intellectual maelstrom, not just of students but of individuals who shaped the political ideas of their own and future generations. Reeve, a devoted and active Federalist, must have participated in or led lively discussions on all manner of topics, ranging from the Revolution (he was an ardent patriot) and the content of the documents which shaped the nation, to the slavery of Elizabeth Freeman and the treason of Aaron Burr. Relaxing in his parlor the benevolent Tapping Reeve may also have dandled the young Harriet Beecher, future author of *Uncle Tom's Cabin*, on his knee.

116, 117 The gathering room at Tapping Reeve
House and (*below*) Mrs. Reeve's downstairs bedroom, added in 1780.

Samuel Morey House and the Ridge

1773-1840

ORFORD, NEW HAMPSHIRE

118, 119 The kitchen of Morey House, with a view through to the dining room and parlor beyond. (*below*) The front entry.

In the pantheon of American inventors some names are instantly recognizable and synonymous with greatness – names like Bell, Franklin, Fulton, Wright, and Edison. But the name of Samuel Morey will probably elicit blank stares, unless you happen to be in that small area of the Connecticut River Valley where during the early part of the nineteenth century this gentleman achieved major miracles with steam.

Samuel Morey's parents were among the first settlers of the town of Orford, New Hampshire. They arrived in 1766 with a group of families from Hebron, Connecticut. Israel Morey was immediately prominent in the new community. He laid out roads, started the first store, the first tavern, and the ferry across the river to Fairlee, Vermont. He also established prosperous business by building the first sawmill and gristmill.

Little did the Moreys know that the frame houses built with their boards were but forerunners to a group of houses which would come to be known as probably the most important group of Federal houses outside a major city. Washington Irving would later say that, "In all my travels in this country and Europe, I have seen no village more beautiful."

Israel Morey owned the Ridge where Orford's distinguished Federal houses would eventually be built. In 1773 he sold the central lot to Obadiah Noble, Orford's first minister, who built the town's first two-story house on the property. Samuel Morey bought back the house and land, added the rear extension in 1800 and in 1804 built the handsome Georgian front which set the standard for the other houses on the Ridge.

The various sections of the Morey House are clearly discernible both inside and out. The 1773 section has classic, narrow, low-ceilinged rooms with handsome eighteenth-century wainscoting and paneling. Much of the paneling, once presumed lost, was uncovered beneath layers of paper and plaster during restoration. The 1804 addition is far more spacious, with a large front stairwell as opposed to the cramped and steep one which has been restored in the older section. The façade is notable particularly for the fine doorway and Palladian window above. The entire house has been painstakingly restored by the present owners, who are long-time Orford residents and historians.

120,121 Samuel Morey House, showing the façade of the 1804 section built by Morey, with its fine doorway and Palladian window above. (*below*) The dining room in the original section of the house, looking through into the parlor.

Samuel Morey grew up in his father's lumber business and ran it during much of his adult life, but the confines of business and the isolation of Orford could not deter him from pursuing his experiments and inventions. He was fascinated by steam power and convinced that it could be harnessed for propulsion of various sorts. His first patent, for a steam-powered cooking spit, came in 1793. Though his wife was probably delighted, and he did enjoy moderate commercial success with it, this invention was much too tame for Morey. He was determined as early as 1790 that he would perfect the steamboat, and he worked on the project persistently.

One Sunday morning in 1792 Morey went down to the river, observed only by some boys who were skipping Sunday meeting, and fired up his steam-powered contraption. He successfully navigated it up and down the river at about five miles per hour. Morey was not the first to experi-

122 The steep stairwell in the old section of the house. This was reconstructed when the house was restored.

123 The entry hall and stairwell of the 1804 section.

ment with the steamboat, but he contributed possibly the most important ingredient to Robert Fulton's eventual triumph. It was Morey who developed the side paddles which proved to be by far the most efficient means of propulsion and navigation. In 1797 he met Robert Livingston, who was most interested in Morey's work. In the end, however, Livingston determined to back Robert Fulton instead of Morey, and in 1807 Fulton's *Clermont*, incorporating Morey's side paddles, steamed up the Hudson. Morey was outraged, but Fulton was legally secure. Morey's patent had not covered the side paddles specifically enough.

Morey went on to other projects far more inventive than Fulton's basically practical and incorporative talents could have managed. Morey's next major accomplishment was his experimentation with water gas, created by the interaction of heated carbon and steam. His house in

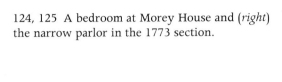

124, 125 A bedroom at Morey House and (*right*) the narrow parlor in the 1773 section.

Orford was the first in America to be heated and lit by water gas. This implementation of the method was fifty years in advance of its use elsewhere in the United States. In what was probably his least known and most inspired moment, Morey developed what Charles Duryea later recognized as the forerunner of the internal combustion engine. Morey adapted this engine to propel a boat, but fell just short of powering a wagon with it.

Morey and his family also owned the choicest piece of real estate in town, and managing this property took up a certain amount of his time. In 1805 he built the house next door, now known as the Wilcox House, for his parents, and he gradually sold off parts of Orford's Ridge as building lots for others. In 1814 he sold the lot on which the Wheeler House was built. This house more than any other has contributed to the myth that has given rise to the Ridge houses being called "Bulfinch Row." None of the houses on the Ridge was built by Bulfinch, the famous Boston architect. Nor were they built according to specific plans by Asher Benjamin, one of Bulfinch's assistants. It does seem, however, that at least Wheeler House was the result of a careful reading of one of the early editions of Benjamin's design book, *The American Builder's Companion*. The final four houses were built between 1817 and 1840.

The overall effect is astonishing. It is important to remember that these gracious houses were not built by summer residents, as in Newport, or by rich urban merchants. They were built by successful members of a small rural community who chose to build handsomely and well. Ironically for Morey, despite all his inventions, the most tangible remembrance of him is probably his house and the others it inspired.

126–128 The Willard House (*left*), 1838–40, was the last of the Ridge houses to be built. It is situated just north of Morey House. The Wheeler House (*right*), 1814–16, one of the finest houses on the Ridge, is the one most clearly identified with the work of Asher Benjamin. Howard House (*below*), 1825–9, is the northernmost of the Ridge houses.

Langdon Mansion

1783-1785

PORTSMOUTH, NEW HAMPSHIRE

John Langdon's political and mercantile accomplishments are those of the consummate patriot businessman. Having protected his fortunes during the Revolution, he thrived in Portsmouth during its heyday following the war. He was born in the town in 1741, and after an apprenticeship as a clerk went to sea. On his return he began to develop his own businesses. By the start of the Revolution he was already an important force in Portsmouth society. Langdon's support for the rebels was unequivocal, and in 1774 he assisted in the munitions raid on the Portsmouth fort, one of the earliest overt revolutionary actions. His clearly articulated patriotism helped him emerge from the Revolutionary period as a figure of national stature.

His outspoken stand was in some ways slightly out of character. Though he was strong and independent, he was also the quintessential conservative in his careful financial dealings. Typical of this attitude was his struggle with John Paul Jones over the funding of *America*. Despite his reputed penuriousness, Langdon entertained sumptuously and the Marquis de Chastellux described him as a "handsome man of noble carriage."

His political credentials are extensive. He was several times Speaker in the Legislature and in 1775 attended the Continental Congress where he served on a number of committees. In 1776 he was placed as agent for Continental Prizes in New Hampshire, an excellent arrangement for Langdon since he had already fitted out a number of privateers. His greatest Revolutionary service came in 1777 when he organized and financed General Stark's expedition against Burgoyne. He participated in the action and was present at the Saratoga surrender. In 1783 he was again in Congress; in 1784 he became a State Senator, and the next year Governor of New Hampshire. He attended the Constitutional Convention in Philadelphia, and after another term as Governor served two terms in the Senate. He retired from that body in 1801, served back in the State Legislature from 1801–5 and then as Governor until 1811, except in 1809 when he actually lost an election. After his final term as Governor he was offered the vice-presidential nomination, which he declined.

Langdon's position in Portsmouth after the Revolution was preeminent. He had managed, even while spending money in support of the rebel cause, to amass a fortune. The house he began in 1783 was designed

129 The impressive ornate entry to Langdon Mansion.

to reflect his prominence both locally and nationally. The first thing that impresses one about the house is its imposing size. It rises in two and a half stories and the exterior embellishments are lavish. The façade is graced with Corinthian corner pilasters, an extremely ornate balustraded portico, dentiled cornices, dormers with scrolled broken pediments above, and a balustrade crowns the steep hipped roof. The house was typical of eighteenth-century Portsmouth houses in its siting. It was set back from the road and surrounded by extensive gardens.

A great deal of the design was drawn from Abraham Swan's *The British Architect* (1745), a venerable text and one of the most ornate of the British pattern books. Its use in a town like Portsmouth is indicative of Langdon's sophistication. The actual construction of the mansion was largely left to Michael Whidden III and Daniel Hart, two Portsmouth shipbuilders who had worked on *America* with Langdon and Jones.

The house is particularly notable for its carving. The designs were undoubtedly derived from Swan, but the execution, while fine, lacks

130 The façade is as graceful and imposing as the rooms behind it.

131 Detail of the fine carving on the overmantel of one of the receiving-room fireplaces.

some of the dimensional aspects of the Swan models. This suggests the work of a local craftsman, who would have had little or no opportunity to view other examples of such work. The identity of the carver is unknown, although Whidden and Hart's itemized bill to Langdon survives. A number of the architectural elements are typical of Portsmouth. The entry way with its arch and stairwell and finely turned balusters is a good example, and reminiscent of the John Paul Jones House.

The layout of the rooms off the central hall follows the standard pattern, except for the parlor, which was clearly built with large entertainments in mind. There is certainly no doubt that Langdon took full advantage of this, as he was known for his gracious parties. He served as host to many of Portsmouth's major visitors, including the Marquis de Chastellux, John Drayton, and, in 1789, George Washington. Washington felt that Langdon's house was the finest in Portsmouth. This was very much a public house, built by a decidedly public man to advertise his position in society. The upstairs rooms bear this out. Only one of them is paneled,   135

132–134 The more ornate of the parlor fireplaces and (*above*) the hallway; (*right*) an upstairs bedroom.

and they are all markedly simpler than the ornate gathering rooms below.

Portsmouth's standing as an international port is obvious from the furnishings and goods Langdon easily procured from points east and south. Window curtains, fabric for the upholstery and the stair carpet all came from England, the china came from France, and the dining chairs from Philadelphia. The wallpapers were probably imported, as in so many fine houses in New England coastal towns.

This is certainly a fine Georgian home. It is a throwback to or a continuation of an earlier stylistic era. John's brother Woodbury Langdon may be said to have built the first great Federal house in Portsmouth, just after his brother's house was completed, but John could have built no other. He was a Revolutionary success, and his house, architecturally the product of one era, made it clear, by its grand, high and public style, that its owner was determined to dominate the next.

During the nineteenth century the house passed out of the family, but in 1907 it was purchased by descendants of Langdon's. They bought back a number of pieces of furniture original to the house, and also commissioned the firm of McKim, Mead and White of New York to build an ell, which includes a fine dining room modeled after the one in Langdon's brother's house.

137

John Brown House

1786-1788

PROVIDENCE, RHODE ISLAND

Chad Browne was the first of generations of Browns to live near the center of Providence life and dominate Rhode Island's commerce. In 1638 he had traveled from Salem to Providence to join Roger Williams' colony known as Providence Plantations. He said he went there to follow his conscience, and one can be fairly certain that his trip from England to Salem had been similarly inspired. He was a surveyor and soon found himself enmeshed in the civil affairs of the new colony. His son John was also a surveyor. It was, however, John's son James who first showed an interest in business concerns, and James's sons James and Obadiah, fourteen years apart in age, who truly established the family business.

James, the elder brother, had interests in navigation, ship building, and trade. In 1725, at the age of twenty-one, he was a partner in and captain of a new sloop called *Four Bachelors* which sailed, apparently most successfully, to the West Indies. The record of Brown's second voyage is more specific. In 1727 he captained *Truth and Delight*, another sloop, to the Indies. He took 11 horses, 15 hogsheads of Indian corn, 16 hundredweight of tobacco, 6 barrels of tar, 12,600 feet of boards, 12,000 shingles, and 700 pounds of cheese. He brought back the inevitable molasses and rum. James died in 1739 at the age of only thirty-five, but the years since he first sailed out of Providence had been productive ones. He had become a highly successful merchant and barterer, spreading the tentacles of his business interests through New England. He also built ships to increase his Caribbean trade, and although he never captained another voyage himself, he found a willing pilot in his younger brother Obadiah, whom James trained in all aspects of the family business.

Obadiah Brown prospered. He continued in the businesses of his brother, but also branched into manufacturing, producing goods as diverse as chocolate and spermaceti candles, one of the family's most profitable products. It was during the middle of the eighteenth century that Providence, largely under the guidance of the Browns, began to challenge Newport for commercial supremacy of Rhode Island.

Obadiah had no sons who survived to adulthood, and so took over the rearing of his brother James's five sons. Another James, the eldest of the five, died in 1750 on a voyage to the Chesapeake, but the remaining four — Nicholas, Joseph, John, and Moses — formed a formidable quartet who dominated Providence's social and commercial life through the latter half

137 View of the John Brown House from the garden.

141

John Brown House

of the eighteenth century. They built up individual businesses, all of which interlocked, either loosely or directly, to create a familial corporation of monolithic proportions. Their interests now encompassed everything from the China trade to iron.

Each of the brothers brought different qualities to the family enterprises, and it was probably this balance that made them so successful. John was the adventurer who always felt that they should be doing more, expanding faster, and spending money to make money. He also refused to desert the slave trade, despite the violent protests of at least one of his brothers. These factors led him to sever direct involvement in the family business in 1771, although he retained an interest in the iron and candle trade and continued to pursue his own business most successfully.

When John decided to build himself a house on Benefit Street, near the new college, of which the Browns were the major benefactors and which would later bear their name, he did something typical of his clan: he asked his brother Joseph, an amateur architect, to design it. Joseph drew his inspiration from various sources, including James Gibbs' *Book of Architecture* and Christopher Wren. Besides his own house (1774), he had designed a number of public buildings prior to turning his hand to his brother's residence, including the First Baptist Meeting House in Providence, the first college building at Rhode Island College (Brown) (1770), and the Market House (1773). The house he designed for his brother was probably his finest work, although he did not live to see it built.

Joseph's creation is a three-story brick mansion with a projecting entry, a Palladian window over the Doric portico, and a hipped and balustraded roof. It is a late Georgian masterpiece, and though similar houses predate it in other American cities, in Providence this was a first. A number of houses of like lines and quality were built nearby during the next few years, and the four that remain comprise one of the finest groups of post-Revolutionary houses in America.

The interior has a classic and simple layout with a large central hallway and paired rooms flanking it. The staircase with its beautiful twisted balusters and intricately twisted newel posts is the first clue that the detailing in this house is exceptionally fine, in fact it is second to none. The shadow rail ends in a spiral, a hallmark of Joseph Brown's work. This kind of treatment of a stairway was old-fashioned by the time Brown employed it. Antoinette Downing in her article on the house implies that Brown probably used the style to mimic and outstrip the fashion of the earlier mansions of the Newport merchant princes, which suggests there was still a certain amount of rivalry between the two towns.

The design books used for interior detailing were not the latest, but they included some of the best, such as Gibbs' (1728), Abraham Swan's *Designs* (1745), Batty Langley's *Builder's Compleat Assistant* (1738), and William Salmon's *Palladio Londonensis*. Doors and overmantels are routinely topped with broken scrolled pediments, archways are supported by Ionic columns, interior shutters fold into handsome embrasures, and all the downstairs moldings have remarkable detail. The upstairs detailing,

142

138, 139 The main stairwell from the back of the house and (*right*) detail of the banister and shadow-rail.

while somewhat simpler, follows very similar lines. Eleven of the twelve mantelpieces are original, the paint colors and wallpapers have been restored. Pilasters abound; the two flanking the southeast parlor entrance are topped by marble busts bought for the house by John Brown. The house has been magnificently and appropriately furnished by the Rhode Island Historical Society, which owns and maintains it.

After John Brown's death in 1803 the house passed out of the Brown family for some time. In 1936 John Nicholas Brown bought it from the estate of Marsden Perry. He later gifted it to the Historical Society. Happily, during the house's varied career, though additions were made, no irreversible damage was done to the central original structure. When Abigail Adams, who as we have seen was never quite satisfied with the size and stature of her house in Quincy, visited the Brown House in 1789 she said that "Everything in and about it wore the marks of magnificence and taste." Her son John Quincy Adams was even more lavish in its praise and wrote in his diary that it was "the most magnificent and elegant private mansion that I have ever seen on this continent."

140, 141 The southwest parlor of the John Brown House. Note the squirrel in the broken pediment over the mantel. (*above*) Detail of the carving over the dining-room doorway.

142, 143 The main entry hall of the John Brown House and (*left*) the southeast parlor, looking into the dining room.

145

Harrison Gray Otis House

1795

BOSTON, MASSACHUSETTS

To be absolutely correct this house should be called the first Harrison Gray Otis House as it is the first of three important houses built in Boston by Otis. Otis did not live in it very long. He did, however, leave his mark on the house, mainly through his choice of Charles Bulfinch as the architect. He built it in 1795, served in Congress from 1797 to 1801, and on his return to Boston proceeded to build a new house on Mt. Vernon Street on Beacon Hill.

A 1783 Harvard graduate, Otis was a prominent Boston lawyer passionately devoted to politics. If regional jingoism is possible then that is what he personified. He led the Federalist party during its waning years and was a constant champion of Northern supremacy. His dearest wish was to "snatch the sceptre from Virginia forever." His hopes for true national prominence were dashed in 1814 when he was largely responsible for convening the disastrous Hartford Convention. The failure of this gathering spelled doom for Otis' political ambitions and for his beloved Federalists. But he lived on until 1848, enjoyed a most successful career, and was in every way the quintessential aristocratic Bostonian.

When Otis decided to build a house on his property on Cambridge Street, a gift from his father-in-law, he turned to Boston's best and first truly professional architect, Charles Bulfinch. Bulfinch's contribution to American architecture was monumental. In Boston he designed and built such major projects as the State House (1799), the Federal Street Theater (1794), University Hall at Harvard (1815), Massachusetts General Hospital (1820), as well as placing his indelible stamp on the Beacon Hill district. He was chosen in 1820 to succeed Benjamin Latrobe as architect of the Capitol, and it was Bulfinch who finally saw that project through to completion. When Bulfinch accepted Otis' commission he had already completed the Federal Street Theater, but at thirty-two was still at the beginning of his long and illustrious career.

Bulfinch drew his style from classical roots, and though the exterior of the Otis house is somewhat atypical in its severity, the interior is classic Bulfinch. He was largely responsible for introducing to New England the classical influences on architecture made popular by the Scotsman

Robert Adam. This influence is evident throughout the Otis house. The ornaments on the dining-room mantels, for instance, are identical to ones found elsewhere in America and in England. In the fashion of the Adams these details were usually reproduced in bright contrasting colors.

A brilliant and even startling sense of color is in fact the first thing that strikes one when wandering through the Otis house. Everywhere one looks there is a bright yellow or a classic blue and even pink heightening on ceiling molding in the upstairs parlor. The house in its restored state makes a definitive statement about New England high style taste at the turn of the eighteenth century.

Retrieving these remarkable colors was no easy task. The house went through various owners prior to its acquisition and restoration by the Society for the Preservation of New England Antiquities in 1916. These

144 Detail of carving on the dining-room fireplace.

146–148 The upstairs withdrawing room (*below*) with its mirrored mahogany doors; (*bottom*) the front entryway and (*right*) a view from the withdrawing room looking through two bedrooms.

various incarnations left behind the usual and seemingly impenetrable layers of paint and paper. Careful peeling and scraping down to the original plaster was not in itself sufficient. The paint colors uncovered did not correspond with any documentation contemporary with the completion of the house.

In recent years the technology for paint analysis has improved dramatically and has been used to great effect in a number of houses presented in this book. In the Otis House all available techniques were applied. Chemical and spectrographic analyses revealed that a glaze had been used to heighten the glossy finish when the rooms were first painted. This glaze then turned brownish-yellow with age. When this was compensated for it was possible to determine the true original colors and reproduce them. Thus the exquisite details in the fireplaces, doorways, and dado were brought back to life, as well as the doors, baseboards, chair-rails and mantel shelves which, it was discovered, had been grained to imitate mahogany.

Restoring the wallpapers was a comparatively easy task. When the layers were removed it was found that the papers next to the plaster were English and bore a tax stamp which dated them in the 1790s. These then must have been Otis' or Bulfinch's original choices. Wherever possible the Society has reproduced them exactly. In the case of the parlor and

149,150 The parlor and next to it a small room probably used as a library and home office, as the safe over the mantel suggests.

the dining room no samples survived so appropriate papers from Henry Knox's home in Thomaston, Maine (believed to have been designed by Bulfinch in 1794), were reproduced.

Another striking feature is the carpeting. Not only do the carpets add yet another layer of brilliant color, but they are also in most instances laid wall to wall, a surprisingly common practice during the period. In his monograph on the house Richard Nylander reminds us that Federal taste in color and design was radically different from our own, and this house speaks eloquently to his point. The overall effect, however, is stunning even though the confluence of color may at first seem jarring to the modern eye.

The nineteenth century was not overly kind to "The Brick House," as Otis called it. The next owner was John Osborn, a paint merchant, who alternately left it vacant while trying to sell it or lived in it and did some redecorating. His daughter finally sold it in 1823, at which point the interior was divided in half. The house served as the home or business establishment for various people, ranging from a looking-glass maker to one Dr. Mott, who produced patent medicines. The venerable building saw the turn of the nineteenth century in the guise of a rooming house. The Harrison Gray Otis House now reigns as the only remaining free-standing townhouse in Boston.

151 Harrison Gray Otis House on Cambridge Street, aptly called "The Brick House" by Otis.

152 The doorway of Harrison Gray Otis House.

153 The doorway of Gardner-Pingree House.

153

Gardner-Pingree House

1804-1805

SALEM, MASSACHUSETTS

On August 6, 1830, the Gardner-Pingree House was the scene of a most dastardly crime. Joseph White, a wealthy Salem merchant was asleep on the second floor of the mansion in Essex Street when three young men stole up the stairs and murdered him. They were apparently trying to forestall White from cutting them out of his will. Joseph Knapp and John Francis Knapp, distant relations of the elderly White, and Richard Crowninshield were arraigned for the crime. Crowninshield committed suicide in jail after being accused by Joseph Knapp. The Knapps were tried for murder, convicted and hanged. Daniel Webster served as the prosecutor. Rarely had a group of young murderers picked such a handsome place to commit such an ugly crime.

The murder was big news in Salem where sensational happenings, while not commonplace, are not exactly unheard of. The town was founded in 1626 and the first Congregational Church was organized there in 1629. One of the earliest of its pastors was Roger Williams. The fact that the town is most noted for religious intolerance and the witchcraft trials of 1692 tends to obscure its position as one of New England's leading and most interesting maritime and shipbuilding centers. The port served as a privateer base in both the Revolution and the War of 1812, and Salem's active commerce produced many a fortune during the eighteenth and nineteenth centuries. The houses these mercantile fortunes built still line the streets of the town. White's house had been built by Samuel McIntire for John Gardner, another Salem merchant. It is one of the finest houses in a town famous for its fine architecture, particularly of the late Georgian and Federal periods.

John Gardner was the product of an extremely successful mercantile clan. He was a grandson of Richard Derby, one of Salem's famous captains from the early days. By the end of the eighteenth century Gardner had built up a solid import business and, like many others in town, saw the construction of an elegant mansion house as an appropriate display of his success. He chose Samuel McIntire, Salem's greatest architect, to design it.

Just as Charles Bulfinch changed the face of Boston through his dominance of the architectural scene, so McIntire influenced the building style in Salem. By the time he was in his twenties he had demonstrated an architectural intelligence far beyond his years. He had also earned the support and patronage of one of Salem's greatest merchants, Elias Hasket

Derby. He designed and built many houses in Salem, including the Pierce-Nichols house (*c.* 1782), the Clifford Crowninshield house (1815), and of course Mr. Derby's house on Derby street. Among the important houses McIntire built outside Salem are Oak Hall in Peabody, Massachusetts (1801–4), and the Lyman House in Waltham, known as "The Vale" (1793). He also designed a number of commercial buildings in Salem, including the Assembly House (1782) on Federal Street.

Probably McIntire's greatest skill was as a carver, so when Bulfinch introduced the intimate design features of the brothers Adam to Boston, McIntire instantly recognized a style to which he was naturally attuned. (Like the Adams McIntire made furniture as well.) The Gardner-Pingree House is considered by many to be the apex of his mature architectural style. It is an extremely elegant residence. The exterior is typically Federal, with the ornamentation limited to stringcourses delineating the stories, a roof-line balustrade, dentiled cornices, and a portico ornately decorated with both Corinthian columns and pilasters.

The interiors are classic McIntire at the height of his powers. The original mantels were miraculously saved by the Pingrees when they replaced them during the nineteenth century. They have since been

154 The dining room.

155–157 Gardner-Pingree House on Essex Street in Salem. (*below*) An upstairs bedroom and (*right*) the parlor. The carving over the doorway is the work of McIntire.

158, 159 The entry hall and detail of the balustrade.

re-installed. The design motifs include Corinthian columns, swags, rosettes, sheaves of wheat, and McIntire's signature – a basket of fruit. The arch in the double parlor repeats these motifs. Many of the interior cornices are dentiled. The interior layout is typically Federal and quite similar to the first Harrison Gray Otis house. Like that house it is notable for the wall-papers, installed during restoration. The house has been handsomely furnished to reflect the international nature of Salem's commerce. The Essex Institute, which restored the house and now owns and maintains it, is in the process of further research in this area.

During the War of 1812 John Gardner's business was troubled and in order to resurrect his fortune he attempted a daring trading voyage to Europe. Unfortunately, he was captured just short of a safe return and taken to Halifax, an eventuality against which he was not insured. This and other setbacks forced him to sell his mansion house to his brother-in-law Nathaniel West, who rented it to Gardner. Although Gardner's fortunes improved, they never approached their previous height, and he moved out of his house in 1815 after West sold it to James White.

After White's unfortunate demise his nephew Stephen, who inherited, found it quite difficult to sell the house, doubtless because of its notoriety. In 1834, however, he sold the mansion to David Pingree, though the purchase price of only $7000 was certainly low. Another Salem merchant with worldwide interests, Pingree had a mixed business career, and left behind a troubled estate when he died in 1848. His son David, through careful shepherding of the family's affairs, managed to revivify the fortune. The major source of his success was his vast holdings of real estate in Maine, which totaled 700,000 acres. Pingree was the largest individual landowner in New England. He was a committed bachelor and a generous, quiet philanthropist. His heirs gave the house to the Essex Institute.

160, 161 These elegant
rooms at Gore Place echo
the gracious exterior.
The bowed walls of the
morning room (*top*) reflect
the shape of the main
state rooms.

Gore Place

1805-1806

WALTHAM, MASSACHUSETTS

On the night of March 19, 1799, the frame house which Christopher Gore had built on his estate outside Boston burned to the ground. No one was injured (Gore was in England at the time and his brother-in-law was living in the house), and some of the furniture was saved, though it was badly damaged. It was in a way a fortunate mishap for had it not been for the fire the magnificent house that was raised on the old site would never have been constructed. This house, Gore Place, is unquestionably one of the finest Federal period brick mansions in America.

Christopher Gore was, by any standards, a man of many parts. After graduating from Harvard in 1776 and serving in the Revolution he read law in Judge John Lowell's office. He soon started his own Boston practice and specialized in mercantile law, numbering among his clients some of London's most prosperous firms. His influence was destined to spread much further than the business world alone. In 1788 he served as a member of the Massachusetts convention which ratified the Federal Constitution. George Washington then appointed him District Attorney for Massachusetts in 1789, and in 1794 he was appointed chief negotiator on the London Claims Commission pursuant to the Jay Treaty. He served in London for eight years, alongside his lifelong friend Rufus King.

When he returned to Boston in 1804, Gore reopened his law practice and became more active in politics. In 1806 and 1807 he served in the Massachusetts Senate and then in the House of Representatives. He was elected Governor of Massachusetts in 1809 but retired after one term and tended to his estate in Waltham. He returned to public life as a United States Senator between 1813 and 1816, then the decline of the Federalists as well as his health prompted his permanent retirement.

Although Gore may not have been a pivotal figure in the Revolutionary or Federal periods, we can to some extent judge his influence by the company he kept. He numbered among his friends and associates such luminaries as John Hancock, Samuel Adams, Royall Tyler, Thomas Dawes, Reverend James Freeman, Fisher Ames, John Trumbull, and John Singleton Copley. The fact that these last two were painters is no accident: Gore took an active interest in the artists of his day. Trumbull's portrait of Gore hangs in the house and Copley's portrait of two of the Gore children hangs in the family dining room. Gore also took an interest in education and he enjoyed the company of students. There are many

162 The family dining room. The Copley portrait of two of the Gore children hangs over the mantel.

stories telling of Harvard students walking out to Waltham from Cambridge and spending a delightful summer day with the Gores. The visits generally ended with a trip to the billiard room and a carriage ride home. This generous and influential country squire had much to be proud of, but his beginnings were less than grand: he was the eighth of thirteen children born to a Boston carriage painter.

Very little is known about the early frame structure of Gore's first Waltham house. After it had burned down Gore and his wife Rebecca Payne, daughter of the President of the First Bank of Massachusetts, went right to work planning a replacement. In 1801 while on a trip to Paris they met a prominent French architect named Jacques Guillaume Legrand. Legrand had designed a number of residences and was the author of several architectural handbooks and guides. He particularly impressed Mrs. Gore, who took a great interest in the design for the new house. After her return to London she sent on a specific series of guidelines and Legrand was requested to draw up plans. Legrand's direct involvement

163 The north side of Gore Place with its fine
Federal façade.

in the design of Gore Place has been questioned in the past, but the
evidence that he was rather more than a consultant is mounting.

Regardless of the exact role of those involved the alchemy was certainly
splendid. The exterior of Gore Place, though simple, is graceful. The
house was built in three basic sections, a two-story central core flanked
by matching wings. The north façade, the side from which the house is
approached and entered, is dominated by a raised stone porch, tall first-
floor windows, and two entry doors. The doorways are fine examples of
Federal detail, and the shape of the fanlights is repeated in the lunette
windows, which light the mezzanines of the wings. The wings have
rectangular end pavilions, the planes of which are broken by twice-
recessed walls, suggesting pilasters. This handsome understatement is
typical of the house both inside and out.

The south façade is different in one major respect. On this side most of
the central portion of the house is bowed dramatically, with triple hung
windows on the ground floor looking out over Gore's property. The

effect is stunning, and the bow of the rear façade gives rise to some of the most interesting interior lines of the house.

The entry hall, reached through the left-hand porch door, features one of the most famous stairwells in New England. The hanging staircase is breathtaking from every angle and its graceful curves are only a hint of what is to come. The floor, made of three different shades of gray American marble, continues into the main reception hall, one of the state rooms in the central core. The front wall of this room is flat, but the rear one is curved, a mirror image of the wall of the elliptical state dining room, so curved because of the bow in the south façade. These dramatic curves and spirals give the house a most unusual flavor.

The remainder of the central portion of the house comprises a family dining room and morning room below and the family parlor and bedrooms above. In a number of these rooms the original wallpapers have been reproduced magnificently. The west wing contained servants' quarters and the kitchen (Gore had every modern convenience, including a full bathtub). The billiard room where Gore's friends, including his famous law clerk Daniel Webster, used to gather is in the east wing. Gore's library was housed in the end pavilion. The mezzanine contains the nursery, one of the most charming rooms in the house, and the children's bedrooms.

Christopher Gore lived in the house until his death in 1827 at the age of sixty-eight. His wife died in 1834 and the house was sold. It is now maintained by the Gore Place Society, which was formed to save the property from development after long service as a golf course and club house. Today the house stands as a reflection of the couple who built it – comfortable but also elegant, graceful but straightforward, grand but generous.

164, 165 South front of Gore Place, clearly showing the three sections of the house. The shutters are closed as they would have been during much of the hot summer weather. (*right*) The entry hall with its delicately wrought staircase. The door opens on to the main reception room.

167 The children's room in the east wing
mezzanine at Gore Place. Light floods in through
the lunette window.

Florence Griswold House

1817

OLD LYME, CONNECTICUT

Arthur Heming, a Canadian painter, illustrator, and writer, wrote a delightful memoir of his times at Florence Griswold's house. His initial impression has a special appeal. He speaks of knocking at the front door of Miss Florence's magnificent house. Receiving no answer, he opened the door, and stepped into the front hall.

> Then I looked around. There I saw two old sofas that had gouged holes in the wall plaster with their restless backs, while their wobbly legs seemed to be vainly reaching out after their runaway casters, as several cats and dogs slept soundly . . . The drawing room door being open I entered. Its ancient air was something like the hall, only a little worse. Reposing under the broken seat of a handsome old armchair was a pile of big books to prevent guests from bumping the floor when they sat down. Another pile of books, snuggling under one corner of a splendid old chesterfield, substituted for a missing leg. . . . Many other articles of rare old dislocated furniture cluttered the room, and above all rose a beautiful mantelpiece of chaste design. But heaped upon its shelf was a litter of things . . . paint brushes, hat pins, playing cards, pipes, a couple of unfinished sweaters and a lonely toothbrush . . . behind the sofas and other odd pieces of furniture were several beautiful paintings resting against the walls.

This vision of total chaos is not exactly what one is accustomed to finding in historic New England houses. At the same time there is no house with a story quite like that of the Griswold House. It is awkward to place this mansion house in the chronological sequence, not because there is any question concerning its date, but because the most important additions to it and its most glorious era came more than seventy-five years after the house was built. The additions did not take the usual form of ells or roofs or even wainscoting or carving. The additions were paintings done by some of the finest American painters of the Barbizon and Impressionist schools. The artists came to Old Lyme in the summers to paint in a colony founded by Henry Ward Ranger and always hosted by the cheery, if slightly mad, Florence Griswold.

When Florence's father, Captain Robert Griswold, bought the house in 1841, he certainly could never have envisaged the strange goings-on which eventually filled the rooms of his imposing dwelling. The house was built by William Noyes in 1817, although what is now the rear ell is actually an eighteenth-century structure. The far larger 1817 portion was designed by Samuel Belcher, a Hartford-born architect who was also the designer of the John Sill House and the First Congregational Church in Old Lyme. The late Georgian façade is impressive, and the detailing superb. Corner quoins, a central Palladian window, a deep dentiled cornice, and the handsome large portico add to the massive effect.

The interior, while not exquisite, is fine and strong. Many of the rooms are now given over to gallery space, but the downstairs has a number of period rooms, including the front parlor, Miss Florence's bedroom, and

168, 169 Painted panels in the dining room. The top one shows the façade of the house. (*below*) Florence Griswold House.

the dining room where the artists gathered for their meals (except for the members of the "Hot Air Club," who preferred the porch in the ell during the hottest weather).

Captain Griswold was a prosperous packet-boat captain, but after his death his wife and daughters were in precarious financial straits. In order to make ends meet they opened up a finishing school in the house, but it was never very successful. In 1899, when Henry Ward Ranger first arrived at her door, Miss Florence was the only remaining family member, and the house was a little dilapidated. Undaunted, Ranger proceeded to establish a summer art colony of fellow Barbizon school painters. The surroundings were ideally suited for the project, blending man and nature in the Barbizon fashion, and Miss Florence provided perfect living accommodation, if a bit rustic, as barns became studios. For the next twenty years artists came to Old Lyme, and Miss Florence set the table, charging them about nine dollars a week for room and board.

Miss Florence was not beautiful, but by all accounts she was charming. She was forever in debt, largely as a result of extending credit to artists who were, to put it delicately, between sales. Her house was basically as Arthur Heming described it, a cluttered mess, but it fit her personality as well as that of her tenants. She numbered Woodrow Wilson among her friends. He spent parts of the summers of 1905, 1909, and 1910 with her, a rare exception to the artists-only rule. Wilson stopped on the Presidential yacht to see Miss Florence in 1915, and remembered her and his experiences at the colony fondly until his death.

The atmosphere in the house was as chaotic as the furnishings, and practical joking was commonplace. Townspeople and visitors soon discovered that an excursion to Miss Florence's house to view the artists at

170 Side view of Griswold House with the famous porch where many of the artists took their meals in the hot summer weather.

171, 172 Florence Griswold's bedroom and (*right*) the entry hall. The placement of the stairwell is interesting since it is not typical of houses of this style.

their work was an interesting experience, but they were sometimes greeted oddly. One evening Miss Florence was making dinner when some gawkers arrived. She explained that the artists were indeed there, and if the visitors would wait they could even see them eat. She rang the bell and the men, obviously having overheard her, came tearing down the hall on all fours, snarling, snapping, and growling like starving carnivores.

Artistically the colony diversified. Prior to 1903 Ranger and other Barbizon naturalists reigned, but after that Childe Hassam, who gleefully referred to the tonalists' work as the "Brown Gravy School," arrived and injected his own American Impressionism. Not only did Hassam attract artists such as Walter Griffin, but members of the Barbizon school experimented with their styles. From 1903 to 1920 the artists who had worked during the summer exhibited in town. During these years more than eighty artists of varying importance were represented in the exhibitions, and many of their works are now on view in the house.

Some of the most interesting paintings are not hanging on the walls, but literally painted on them. Over the years the tradition of painting door panels developed, and later Miss Florence provided additional panels in the dining room for further embellishment. The effect is extraordinary. Perhaps the finest panel in the dining room is the delightful one under the mantel, by Henry R. Poore, which shows the colony artists at work and play around Old Lyme. Hassam, Ranger, William Robinson, Henry Heming, Edward Rook, Will Howe, Carleton Wiggins, and Allen B. Talcott are all depicted.

Miss Florence lived in the house until her death in 1937, by which time a fund had been established to maintain it. The mansion is now the headquarters of the Old Lyme Historical Society.

173–175 (*left*) The dining room of Griswold House. The panel over the fireplace depicts the Old Lyme artists at work and at play; (*right*) details of the panels in the dining room and parlor. William H. Howe's *The Monarch of the Farm* (*below*) is one of the most famous.

Kingscote

1840-1841

NEWPORT, RHODE ISLAND

So far in these pages we have looked at two Newport houses: the Wanton-Lyman-Hazard House and Hunter House. These two houses are typical of the early part of Newport's history when the town was a bustling trading center. Kingscote, on the other hand, represents the beginnings of an entirely different tradition for this lovely coastal town. It was the first of the great Bellevue Avenue cottages, and its building ushered in the grand era of Newport's summer seasons.

Newport had been a summer haven for Southerners even in the eighteenth century, but after the Revolution the town changed drastically. It never regained its mercantile station, and for a time the summer population almost disappeared. During the first quarter of the nineteenth century some of the summer families gradually began to return, but they mostly rented homes or stayed in one of the few fashionable guest houses. It was not until the 1830s and '40s that the building of substantial summer cottages began.

When George Noble Jones, a Georgian well connected with the Southern summer community, bought property on a dirt road well beyond the outskirts of town, eyebrows must have been raised, just as eyebrows in New York were raised when James Renwick was commissioned to build St. Patrick's Cathedral outside the city limits. Luckily for Jones his decision proved as perspicacious as that of the archdiocese; the street later became Bellevue Avenue in one of the town's most elegant areas.

Jones chose Renwick's fellow exponent of the Gothic Revival Richard Upjohn as his architect, largely because Upjohn had built his wife's family home in Maine. Jones asked Upjohn to build him a cottage with eight bedrooms, and specially requested that the waterclosets and bath be inside.

When looking at Kingscote it is important to remember that the house as it now appears is somewhat different from its original configuration. The addition, or more properly the insertion, of the Stanford White wing in 1881–2 changed the overall lines of the house. If you imagine the house without the highest of its roof-lines, and move the rear wing up in line with the rest of the building (see the photograph of the façade), you can begin to see the house as Upjohn designed it.

Upjohn's devotion to the Gothic Revival was absolute, and Kingscote is a *cottage orné* of the highest style. The drip moldings over the windows,

176 The playroom at Kingscote. The Gothic windows look out over the front lawn.

177 Side view of Kingscote. The porch runs along the outside wall of the double parlor.

a motif continued throughout the interior, the variegated drop tracery under the eaves, the cross tracery in some of the upper windows, and the occasional crenelation are all typical of the style. The interior of the old part is equally highly styled, and includes many a Tudor arch, deeply coved moldings, and a number of curved interior walls.

The "season" as it is now known in Newport was not so clearly defined in the early nineteenth century. Vacationers might come for just a few weeks or arrive in early spring and not leave until late fall. There were plenty of parties, but social life tended to revolve more around a main meal taken in mid-afternoon and an evening of charades and other games. The mornings were usually given over to horseback riding on the beach.

Prior to the Civil War and despite the influx of many Bostonians on the summer scene, the atmosphere in Newport was markedly Southern. Needless to say the Civil War changed this forever. Many Southerners feared the confiscation of their property, and George Jones protected his by selling it to his sister who was then living in Montreal. In 1863 she sold the house, for $35,000, to William Henry King, whose brother Edward had been a neighbor since the 1840s.

The Kings had been a prominent Newport family since the end of the eighteenth century, and William and Edward had both made successful careers in the China trade. Upjohn had built an Italianate villa for Edward 175

just to the west of the Jones house and it seemed ideal that William should settle nearby. The furniture and paintings which William had collected in China came with him, and much of this collection still remains in Kingscote, along with a few pieces which date back to the Jones era.

Unfortunately, this happy family arrangement was not destined to flourish long. In 1866, after only two years in the house, William King suffered a mental collapse and was institutionalized for the remaining thirty-one years of his life. He never returned to Newport and the court appointed a series of relatives to oversee and live in Kingscote. The first of these relatives were William's brothers George and Edward, neither of whom took a great deal of interest in the house. In 1875, following Edward's death, the trusteeship fell to their nephew David whose wife, Ella Louisa Rives King, took a real liking to the cottage. Her interest and energy carried the house through various upgradings and two renovations. David and Ella's descendants lived in the house until 1972 when it was left to the Preservation Society of Newport County.

The first renovation is interesting because it remains almost undetectable, and the second is equally so because it changed the house dramatically. The first was done by the famous Newport architect George Champlin Mason who, with religious devotion to Upjohn's work, enlarged the dining room and made an addition to the servants' wing. Almost all evidence of this renovation was obliterated when in 1881–2 McKim, Mead and White were commissioned to design a new wing, which was

179 The removable screen at the east end of the Stanford White dining room.

to include a massive new dining room more in keeping with the changing demands of Newport's summer residents. The servants' wing was detached and moved back, and Stanford White's dining room wing inserted between the front and the back of the original house.

White's dining room is remarkable. The floor is cherrywood parquet and the mahogany paneling on the walls rises to the height of the plate-rail. On one wall the paneling is broken to accommodate an enormous built-in sideboard. The east wall is not a wall at all, but rather a removable screen, which reflects the family's involvement in the China trade in its design. The screen allowed for the expansion of the room for use as a ballroom. The west wall has a massive fireplace set off on each side by opaque windows made of Tiffany glass bricks. The windows in the south west wall repeat the motif while the windows above the plate-rail incorporate dahlias in stained glass. These dahlias are repeated in the hall windows beyond the screen. The walls above the plate-rail and the ceiling are tiled in cork. Other changes were made during this period, including the dark graining of the woodworking, the addition of the stained-glass windows at the entry, and the laying of parquet floors in portions of the old house.

Although White's addition does some damage to the purity of Upjohn's Gothic Revival vision, the eclectic nature of the overall effect seems somehow appropriate. Kingscote, with all its various influences, reigns as one of America's nineteenth-century masterpieces.

180, 181 The original dining room at Kingscote, which became a sitting room when the Stanford White dining room was added. (*below*) The entry hall.

182, 183 The southwest corner of the Stanford White dining room and (*below*) looking towards the screen.

Wilcox-Cutts House

1843

ORWELL, VERMONT

The Wilcox-Cutts House, or Brookside as it is locally known, could be called the house that Merino sheep built and Morgan horses maintained. It is undoubtedly one of the most magnificent farmhouses in New England. Not the least of its remarkable qualities is its location. To find a massive Greek Revival mansion two miles from the center of a tiny town in Vermont's Champlain Valley certainly comes as some surprise. It would seem more at home as the county courthouse or on a southern plantation.

In 1788 a Mr. Walker and a Mr. Daily, who had been granted their land in Orwell by Benning Wentworth, sold their shares to William Hollenbeck, who cleared the land and built the first buildings at Brookside farm. The house was a small two-story structure now serving as the ell to the mansion house. The farm, which comprised the house, outbuildings, and 128 acres, was sold by Hollenbeck in 1798 for $1677, a sizable sum in those days. The buyer was a moderately wealthy gentleman from Connecticut via Newport, New Hampshire, named Ebeneezer Wilcox.

Wilcox made a number of changes almost immediately. He moved the house in order to carry out extensive landscaping, and laid out a large park and gardens. (The location of the original cellarhole for the eighteenth-century house is marked out by the urns in front of the Greek Revival façade.) Just after the turn of the century he also added a milking shed and buttery to the original house.

However, the most significant contribution made by Wilcox and his son Linus, who inherited the farm in 1834, was not in the form of landscaping or buildings, but in the introduction of livestock. The Wilcoxes were among the first Americans to raise Spanish Merino sheep, which had been brought back from Europe following Napoleon's Peninsular Campaign. They were introduced to Vermont in 1810. The embargo on imported wool after the War of 1812 enabled the Wilcoxes to make a fortune from their Spanish sheep.

The demand was worldwide and in the 1830s Merinos were sent to Australia to establish the breed there. At that time a prize ram sold for astronomical prices which ranged as high as $15,000. It was this kind of income which allowed Linus Wilcox to conceive and build the massive addition to his house which gives Brookside its present character. The project was given to the aptly named local designer and builder James Lamb, the leading exponent of the Greek Revival in the Champlain Valley.

184, 185 A side view of the Wilcox-Cutts House, clearly showing the early and later sections of the house. (*below*) The hanging staircase.

186–188 The imposing Greek Revival façade of the Wilcox-Cutts House and (*right*) a closer view of the massive pillars. (*left*) The kitchen in the eighteenth-century section of the house.

The style had largely run its course in other parts of New England, but Vermont was, as always, somewhat late in parting with the fashion of the day. Lamb went ahead and created a Greek Revival mansion as grand as any from the first quarter of the nineteenth century.

The addition took thirty men a year to build and cost about $30,000. The workmen were local and the wood was all taken from the farm. At least six varieties were employed: oak, butternut, hemlock, black and white birch, and cherry. Lamb hired Thomas Dake to assist him, particularly on interior details such as the hanging staircase in the front hall. Much of the interior detailing was derived from Minard Lafever and from

189 Detail of the ceiling molding.

190 The parlor has a fine coffered ceiling, shutters, and pilasters.

Asher Benjamin's famous *American Builder's Companion* (Boston, 1827). Lafever was used for the design of the Ionic columns on the façade. These were constructed in a curious fashion. If you look closely you can see that the columns lack the slight bulge in the middle which is usual for this form. The reason for this is that the columns are made up from several pieces of oak. The large trees were cut and lathed on the front lawn and the often irregular pieces were then carefully fitted together. Finally the great columns were strapped together, using much the same system as a cooper would in making barrels.

The gallery is a good example of the fine detailing. The woodwork, set off with delicate rosettes similar to ones found throughout the house, is of black birch, and the magnificent geometrically patterned floor is of black and white birch. The coffered ceilings in the front parlor, the carved hanging staircase, and the rosettes of various forms are all beautifully executed. Many of the wallpapers, including the paper in the parlor, are original.

The workmen labored constantly for the better part of a year. Construction began in the spring and by Thanksgiving the Wilcoxes were able to have their feast in the addition; the interior was completed by Christmas. The Brookside house was certainly the most impressive house in the valley and was the scene of great parties and entertainments.

As the nineteenth century wore on Vermont gradually became less of a center for the woolen trade, and without new blood Brookside might very well have disintegrated. In 1872, however, Linus Wilcox's son-in-law Henry Thomas Cutts inherited the farm. Cutts was a Morgan horse breeder of major importance. He bred fine race horses for thirty years. When J. P. Morgan visited Brookside in 1896 he bought at least a dozen of Cutts' animals. Cutts also raised swine, sheep and cattle, and planted extensive orchards.

The Cutts family made a success of the farm, but the Crash of 1929 erased much of the family fortune. The house stood empty until 1942 when the first of a series of new owners purchased it. It remains in private hands.

191, 192 The hanging staircase and the gallery at
the Wilcox-Cutts House. Note the birch floor.

Morrill Homestead

c.1850

STRAFFORD, VERMONT

Robert Frost thought that there was "no greater name in American education than Justin Smith Morrill," an ironic tribute perhaps to a man whose own education ceased, for lack of funds, at the age of fifteen. Morrill, however, never forgot this deprivation and labored throughout his lengthy career to help others in similar straits.

Born in 1810, Morrill was the eldest of ten children. His father Nathaniel Morrill was a blacksmith and a farmer, and though Justin's mother Mary was an educated woman who inspired his interest in books and education, the family was mainly preoccupied with eking out a living from the sometimes ungenerous countryside around the hamlet of Strafford, Vermont. All the children (only five survived to maturity) worked. Nevertheless, Justin found time to study and read. He also attended the local school and two nearby academies.

Initially it seems strange that he turned down a proffered teaching position, obviously offered as a tribute to his precociousness, in order to accept a job as clerk in the local general store. Morrill, however, knew exactly what he was doing. Not only was the store the center of secular town activity, but it was also owned by Judge Jedediah Harris, whose substantial library became an open sesame for Morrill. Two years later he began a subscription library in town, and at eighteen, his economic future already brightening, he started his own collection, a passion which he never surrendered. Thus Morrill's education was largely of his own making, and though he referred to it as a "moderate" one, his omnivorous reading habits ensured that it was in fact wide-ranging and substantial.

After a brief sojourn in Portland, Maine, to acquire new business skills, Morrill returned to Strafford and went into partnership with his former employer. Their business prospered, as one store became four. After seventeen years, Morrill was in a position to retire. He was still only thirty-eight.

Between 1848 and 1853 Morrill enjoyed a brief and busy retirement. He took a wife and he built his house in Strafford. As it turned out he would see less of this marvelous Gothic Revival homestead than he might have liked. During his years in business and retirement he had developed an active interest in politics, and played a prominent part in many local Whig conventions. He was a disciple of Daniel Webster and proclaimed in later years that Webster "... remains in my memory as the

194–196 The façade of the Morrill Homestead; (*left*) side view and (*right*) the front entry with its stained-glass sidelights.

197, 198 The dining room. The crenelated decoration over the doorways was probably installed when the alterations of 1869 were being carried out, and reflects the differing exterior styles. (*right*) Detail of the painted scenes in the library window.

strongest embodiment of noble appearance, as well as noble accomplishments ... He would perhaps drink too much wine ..." Morrill of course drank none.

In 1854 when the Congressional seat in his district became vacant Morrill was nominated. He served the rest of his life in the United States Congress, twelve years in the House of Representatives and thirty-one in the Senate. He died in 1898 at the age of eighty-eight.

The house he designed and had built during his brief mid-life retirement is a rural delight. Morrill was always interested in architecture, as his long tenure as Chairman of the Senate Building Committee testifies. When he built his house in Strafford he did not turn to a local architect, but rather made sure that the house incorporated the Gothic detailing he desired by taking personal charge of as much of the project as he could. From the ornate finials which top the steeply pitched gabled roof, to the windows and doors which are almost all adorned with moldings, tracery, canopies, railings or pendants, and the elaborate bargeboards under the eaves, this is Gothic Revival dressed to the nines. Morrill attempted to increase the substantial feeling of his relatively small house by painting the flush board siding to simulate sandstone.

In 1869 Morrill made some changes to the residence, including the inevitable addition of a library. He sent to France for a fine hand-painted window, which depicts the ruins of Holyrood Chapel in Scotland, and added the porch entry and the front bay window. These 1869 additions can be easily identified by the crenelated roof-lines they all possess. The crenelated details over the dining-room doors were probably added at the same time. The exterior is also adorned by some remarkable painted

199–201 The kitchen (*left*) and parlor (*right*); (*below*) detail of one of the parlor doors.

window screens which show romantic scenes when viewed from outside; when looking out from within they disappear. The interior of the house is comparatively simple, although some of the detailing is fine. The house is still furnished with many family pieces, in part because it remained in the hands of Morrill's descendants until 1938. It is now owned by the State of Vermont.

Morrill's legislative career was notable for much more than its length, and his concern for American education never flagged. It was Morrill who managed to pass, largely through legislative aplomb and tenacity, the act which established the Land Grant Colleges in the United States. This influx of support for education gave birth to the State university system. In 1888, by obtaining passage of what is known as the Morrill Act, he established the tradition of continued Federal support for these institutions. In his role as Chairman of the Senate Building Committee he oversaw and inspired the construction of many important Federal buildings. The most notable of these combined two of Morrill's greatest abiding interests. The Library of Congress, the building of which he fought for and inspired, may also serve as his most fitting memorial.

The Elms

1901

NEWPORT, RHODE ISLAND

Newport began as a mercantile center, and then became a summer play-ground, first for Southerners and then for the Northeastern elite. During the latter half of the nineteenth century America's new industrial giants began to arrive. Old money mixed with new, and Newport reached its ostentatious height. Its summer season was equal in every way to its winter counterpart, New York. The parties were endless, like the houses. The orgy of construction reached its zenith with mansions like Marble House, The Breakers, and The Elms.

In the nineteenth century America was powered by coal. It has often been said that London's famous fog was at least in part the fault of coal smoke, but it should be remembered that American cities were also so afflicted. Coal heated homes, ran railroads, and powered steam ships. At the turn of the nineteenth century Edward Julius Berwind, who built The Elms, was the king of the American coal industry. He owned more coal properties than any other individual in the United States.

Berwind's success was certainly in the style of Horatio Alger. Born in 1848, the son of German immigrants – his father was a cabinet maker who worked in a piano factory – Berwind's capacity for hard work was obviously acquired early in life. He was rewarded by a Presidential appointment to the Naval Academy (this appointment and his service in the Navy proved useful when he later won the contract to supply all the Navy's coal). In 1874, after his stint in the Navy, Berwind joined forces with his brothers and Judge Alison White to form the Berwind, White Company. Their primary interest was coal mining. When Julius took over the New York office in 1876 he became and remained the undisputed corporate chief. Under his leadership the company did nothing but grow.

At the age of thirty-nine, Berwind married an Englishwoman named Hermione Torrey. The next year he purchased a Newport cottage for summer recreation. Curiously, it was not situated on the waterfront, and it was only a poor wooden relation to the great stone mansion he would later erect. By 1899 he had, at great expense, increased his land holdings around the original cottage and was prepared to build a new residence.

Berwind's choice of architect was intriguing. Rather than turning to one of the established and popular New York firms he chose a Philadelphian, possibly out of loyalty to his home city, named Horace Trumbauer. Like

204, 205 One of many statues which adorn The Elms' terrace. (*right*) The central portion of The Elms from the rear, with the terrace and wide staircase leading to the lawn.

206, 207 A fountain with one of the tea houses in the background and (*above*) a view of the house overlooking the terrace and lawn.

Berwind, Trumbauer was a self-made man. He had joined a prominent Philadelphia firm in 1884, at the age of sixteen, as an office boy. After an eight-year apprenticeship he was ready to set up his own architectural firm. By 1898 he had designed and built three important Philadelphia mansions and the commission for The Elms was forthcoming. His later credits make an impressive collection. They include the Duke mansion in New York, three other houses in Newport (Chetwood, Miramar, and Clarendon Court), the Widener Library at Harvard, and the Philadelphia Museum of Art.

Trumbauer was an inveterate Francophile, although, ironically for one so enamored of things French, he was one of the few architects of his generation not trained in France. Trumbauer's model for The Elms was the Château d'Argenson in Asnières; however, he used this only as a jumping off point. One major distinction between the two is the introduction of far more curves in the lines of the huge windows at The Elms.

This makes for an interesting juxtaposition with the largely rectilinear lines of the building itself.

The exterior of The Elms rises in what appears to be two massive stone stories, but is in fact three. The third story is concealed by a parapet wall which runs along the entire roof-line. It contains sixteen rooms and three bathrooms, all originally designed to house servants. Trumbauer also buried the kitchens and laundry rooms in the sub-basement, along with the heating system which was, of course, coal powered. The coal was delivered from its storage point by trolleys running through tunnels. These design features, as H. H. Reed points out in his monograph on the house, must have given the guests "the impression that the household was run by magic."

Indeed The Elms is magical in many ways. The lovely gardens which spread out behind the house amply compensate for its location away from the shoreline. The majestic rear façade overlooks a spacious terrace dotted with sculpture, with wide steps leading to an open expanse of lawn. At the back of the lawn one finds tea houses, fountains, a sunken garden, and a carriage house and garage which were built in 1911. These buildings had space for ten carriages, six horses, and eight automobiles.

The style of the interior is similar to the grand styles of Marble House or The Breakers, though somewhat more understated. The decorating was overseen by the same French firm as in the other two houses, actually an amalgamation of two great firms, Allard et Fils and Alavoine et Cie. Marble is everywhere – on pillars, pilasters, floors, and even the grand staircase. The gigantic marble table, with its intricately inlaid top, which sits in the second-floor hall, is one of the wonders of the house. Brilliantly colored stone and light dominate the entrance hall and grand

208, 209 The downstairs hall looking toward the library with the grand staircase to the left and the ballroom to the right, and the conservatory, where the Berwinds' daughter Julia spent her afternoons at cards.

210, 211 Detail of the ornate coffered ceiling in the dining room and (*right*) Julius Berwind's bedroom.

staircase. The rooms off the main hall represent a variety of styles, ranging from the cool simplicity of the conservatory to the dark Venetian opulence of the dining room and the chinoiserie of the breakfast room. The overall feeling, however, is French and most of the furniture originally gathered for the mansion (much of which was dispersed in 1962) was Louis XV and XVI. The moldings throughout the house are worthy of note. Though they may appear to have been carved from wood they were actually plastered and then painted or grained by practitioners of a now almost lost art. The library and dining room provide particularly fine examples of this work.

The layout of the house is quite simple. The downstairs centers around the entrance hall and a large ballroom, which leads out to the terrace and gardens. The other gathering rooms are in the north and south wings. Above the ballroom on the second floor is the upstairs living room. The bedrooms in the wings seem simple and small in comparison to the downstairs rooms, as indeed they are, but this is typical of many of the larger Newport cottages, where the emphasis was on party going and giving.

The Berwinds returned from Europe in 1901 to a house which was complete in every detail. The first thing they did was throw a party, highlighted by the release of live monkeys in the garden. This was only the first of many extravaganzas. Over the years the Berwinds became celebrated for their parties: they were sure to provide one on any given Saturday night if none of the other well-heeled denizens of Newport was entertaining on similar scale. Their daughter Julia Berwind lived in the house until her death in 1961, when the property, which was threatened with destruction and development, was acquired by the Preservation Society of Newport County.

212, 213 An elegant corner of The Elms and (*right*) the library. The Madonna and Child over the fireplace is a contemporary copy of one executed by Giovanni della Robbia (1469–1529) for the Church of S. Jacopo di Ripoli in Florence.

Notes and Acknowledgements

Introduction Numerous general sources were useful, but particular thanks go to Abbott Lowell Cummings for his careful research on the early period in his book, *The Framed Houses of Massachusetts Bay 1625–1725*, Harvard University, 1979. The Harriet Thomas quotation appears as quoted in the monograph by Wharton and Lutman on the Wanton-Lyman-Hazard House (see below), and it was this reference which first led me to read Harriet Thomas's work, *Old Houses, with Stories*, Newport, 1928.

Fairbanks House Again thanks to Abbott Cummings, whose *Framed Houses* contains extensive discussion of this house. Also thanks to the Fairbanks Foundation and to the Whites, who serve as caretakers and curators of the house.

Stanley-Whitman House As we went to press a report was being completed which challenges Norman Isham's long-accepted dating of this house. There is no question, however, that the house remains a "first period" house of major importance, even if it is determined that it is of somewhat later date than previously assumed. I have elected to tell the story of the house as it has been related over the last eighty years and await the conclusions of those more expert than myself. For a further discussion of how the importance of the exact date of a house can sometimes be overemphasized see the text on the Gilman Garrison. Many of the things mentioned there also apply in spirit to this case. Dorothy Lunde, Curator of the Farmington Museum (contained in the house), was most helpful. Sources included Lydia Hewes, *A Short History of Farmington*, 1935 (reprinted 1964); Norman Isham and Albert Brown, *Early Connecticut Houses*, 1900 (reprinted 1965), and other printed materials provided by Dorothy Lunde.

Wanton-Lyman-Hazard House Thanks to Dan Snydecker and his able assistants at the Newport Historical Society, and to the monograph by Deborah W. Lutman and Mary Hewes Wharton entitled *The Wanton-Lyman-Hazard House*.

Gilman Garrison The first of many thanks to the staff of the Society for the Preservation of New England Antiquities (SPNEA). The people on site were most cooperative and provided useful reference material. Lyn Spencer, who coordinated our visits, was unfailingly patient and pleasant. Abbot Cummings, then Director of SPNEA, was especially helpful over the complicated issue of the date. Also thanks to Mr. Candy of Maine for his consultation.

Wells-Thorn House The staff of Historic Deerfield could not have been more helpful. My thanks to Director Donald Friary and Curator J. Peter Spang. Mr. Spang's article on the house from *Antiques*, May 1865, was very useful.

Sayward House Thanks to the staff of the Society for the Preservation of New England Antiquities, and to Richard Nylander, Curator of Collections at SPNEA, for his fine article on the house in *Antiques*, September 1979.

Ashley House Thanks again to the staff of Historic Deerfield, particularly Director Donald Friary. Amelia Miller's excellent book on the house, entitled *The Reverend Jonathan Ashley House*, Deerfield, 1962, was invaluable.

Adams Mansion Special thanks to Superintendent Wilhemina Harris and her able assistants who made this visit so delightful. Also to L. H. Butterfield for his excellent article on the house published by the Park Service.

Hunter House First of many thanks to the Preservation Society of Newport County and to all of the people who work in the houses which the Society has so carefully preserved. Monique Pinaggio did a masterful job of coordinating our work in Newport in spite of an unbelievably hectic schedule in midsummer. Sources included Edward Welch, *Hunter House and its Occupants During the Revolutionary War Era*, Newport, n.d.; and Daniel R. Porter and Jane MacLeod Walsh, *The Hunter House. "Mansion of Hospitality"*, published by the Society.

Webb House Thanks to the Colonial Dames and to Kevin McSweeney. Other sources included articles by Susan Watkins on the Webb-Deane-Stevens Museum and Lois Wieder's article on Wethersfield. Both articles appeared in *Antiques*, March 1976. For historical background on the conference I turned to James Thomas Flexner, *George Washington (in the American Revolution) 1765–1773*, Little Brown, 1967, and to Arnold Whitridge, *Rochambeau*, MacMillan, 1965.

Tate House Thanks to the Colonial Dames, and to Frances Peabody, whose fine volume, written together with William David Barry, entitled *Tate House. Crown of the Maine Mast Trade*, Portland, 1982, was invaluable.

John Paul Jones House Thanks to Colonel Wesley Ackroyd, President of the Portsmouth Historical Society, and the charming on-site help of his assistants at the house. They provided much useful printed material. Background information came from Samuel Eliot Morison's biography of Jones published by Little Brown, 1959.

Tapping Reeve House Thanks to the Litchfield Historical Society and to its Director Jerry Carroone.

Samuel Morey House and the Ridge Alice Doan Hodgson and her husband own the Morey House. Mrs. Hodgson is also

Orford's resident and foremost historian. Their careful advice and counsel were irreplaceable. Mrs. Hodgson generously provided me with two of her monographs, *Orford, New Hampshire. A Most Beautiful Village*, Littleton, 1978, and *Samuel Morey. Inventor Extraordinary*, Orford, 1961.

Langdon Mansion Once again thanks to the staff of SPNEA. Lyn Spencer provided me with some excellent material, including Barbara Cleary's article on the house, which appeared in the Summer-Fall 1978 edition of SPNEA's *Old Time New England*, and John Cornforth's article about Portsmouth houses from *Country Life*, May 1979.

John Brown House Thanks to the staff of the Rhode Island Historical Society. Antoinette Downing's article in *Antiques* of May 1965, when the house was undergoing restoration, was very useful, as was James Hodges' book, *The Browns of Providence Plantations*, Cambridge, 1952.

Harrison Gray Otis House Thanks again to Lyn Spencer and SPNEA. This time particular help was given by Richard Nylander both in person and through his article on the Otis House in *Antiques*.

Gardner-Pingree House The Director of the Essex Institute, Bryant Tolles, was most generous in allowing us to photograph the interior of the house. The Institute's Curator, Dean Lahikoenan, was also very helpful. My major printed source was Gerald Ward's fine monograph on the house published by the Institute in 1976.

Gore Place Charles Hammond, Director of the Gore Place Society, was extremely charming and helpful during our visit, and he provided some very useful information regarding the architect. I also consulted Peter Wick's December 1976 article in *Antiques*.

Florence Griswold House Jeffrey Andersen, Director of the Old Lyme Historical Society and a specialist on the artists of the colony, made himself available at all times. Other sources were the articles, including that of Mr. Andersen, in *Old Lyme. The American Barbizon*, Old Lyme, 1982; John Tarrant's article in *Smithsonian*, January 1982; and the marvelous reprint of Arthur Heming's memoir, *Miss Florence and the Artists of Old Lyme*, 1971, from which I was generously given permission to quote liberally in my text.

Kingscote Monique Pinaggio and her on-site assistants at the Preservation Society of Newport County were as always very helpful. J. Walter Ferguson's monograph on Kingscote, published by the Society in 1977, was most useful.

Wilcox-Cutts House Many thanks to the Korda clan who are presently struggling with upkeep of this massive and marvelous house. We had a most pleasant visit and they supplied much useful material, including George Gallenkamp and Richard Wunder's article from *Antiques*, June 1979. (Mrs. Korda is refitting one of the outbuildings in hopes of taking guests.)

Morrill Homestead Thanks to Mrs. Lewis, who let us roam so freely with cameras, and to Gertrude Mallary, who put me onto the house and played some part in its preservation. Other sources included William Belmont Parker, *The Life and Public Service of Justin Smith Morrill*, Boston, 1924, and an article in *MD Medical News*, February 1978, entitled "American Gladstone" with no notation of authorship.

The Elms The Preservation Society of Newport County again provided help and information and Henry Hope Reed's monograph on the house published by the Society was most useful.

Acknowledgements are a dangerous business. At every stop on this project Graydon and I received universally excellent assistance and to single out any one organization would be extremely difficult. In the Notes above I have listed the books, monographs, and individuals whose ideas were tapped to write the text. Without this kind of assistance this book would have been absolutely impossible.

A few friends whose help deserves special mention must be included here. Lindy Whiton of Greenfield, Massachusetts, belongs first and foremost. Without her help the hotel and car rental bills would have finished the project when less than half done, and without the Greenfield household's friendly support I would certainly have lost my mind. Lindy let me take her car a long way toward a blown engine – now, I fear, a reality. Also thanks to GRM, EPM, and Myrtle, who lent similar invaluable support, to Frances Neville-Rolfe, who served as principal reader, and to Cathy's magic fingers.

Finally, I would like to thank the staff of the New York Society Library and the ever patient staff of John Calmann & Cooper Ltd, particularly Laurence King and Diana Davies. A last heartfelt thanks to Abbott Lowell Cummings, whose assistance was critical to the proper completion of this work.

Index